thanks
everythi

Tom Sprague

From Poverty

to Glory

Growing up in the Great Depression

... a time when children could be children, free to roam the countryside, be one with nature, and at peace with themselves and God.

Thomas Sprague Sr.

Times were hard

---

their spirits were strong

Published by White Feather Press, LLC in 2008

ISBN   978-0-9766083-6-3

Printed in the United States of America

White Feather Press

Reaffirming Faith in God, Family, and Country!

"From Poverty to Glory paints a warm picture of a time of familial strength and happiness in the midst of financial hardship. This engaging story of rural children growing up during the great depression takes them through frequently amusing but always compelling adventures where they learn that the love of God, family, and friends buys far more than dollars ever will. Here you'll find life lessons often forgotten but still needed in our fast-paced technological age."

Rex M. Rogers
Former President, Cornerstone University

"Truly a light-hearted book on a serious subject, that reads like a modern-day Huckleberry Finn tale."

Joseph Aller
CPA, Former Publisher

Foreword

This is a story of growing up during the Great Depression of the 1930s, a story of brothers and sisters, parents and grandparents, together under one roof, a story of family, neighbors, and community.

But in a greater sense, it is the story of every youngster who lived through that era. Each reader will find his own story here as well: stories of imaginary play trucks, pretend cars, and of making do; reminiscences of the one-room schoolhouse, the disciplinarian teacher and parental involvement; remembrances of barefoot summers, cardboard shoe repairs and hand-me-downs.

Tom Sprague's book speaks of a time when children were never without something to do; a time of learning from experience (not always pleasant) of accepting responsibilities, and being responsible; a time of learning to tell a good story by listening to grandfather's tales and learning to separate fact from fiction in those same stories. It was a time when a boy with good aim could feed the cats directly from the cow!

For the younger reader, it is a picture of what once was, but will never be again, a time that now exists only in memory.

Enjoy.

Harold F. Nye
Barry County Michigan Historical Society

Introduction

Was the Great Depression just a time of dreary days and gray spirits between the Roaring Twenties and the mobilization for World War II? Not at all! My desire is to capture the spirit of the rural people during the Great Depression and show their inner strength when faced with overwhelming financial hardships. Even more than that, I want to show how families and communities worked together for the benefit of everyone.

Farming was a very labor-intensive occupation and often jobs like thrashing required all the neighbors to work together to accomplish the harvest. Without this cooperation many fields of grain would have been lost to the elements. Wheat, for instance, would begin to grow if it got wet after it had ripened. Corn under wet conditions will mold in the field if too much moisture stays in the husk for a prolonged period. To accomplish this harvest it required several men with horse-drawn wagons to haul the grain to the thrashing machine. Several more men were required to operate the thrashing machine itself and to care for the grain and straw. There was no way one farmer could do this alone, so the thrashing crew, made up of the neighboring farmers, traveled from farm to farm until everyone's crops were harvested. When sickness or tragedy befell someone, the community would gather around to do the necessary chores and field work until that family could function again. This dependence forged strong community bonds.

Siblings supported each other and looked out for the welfare of one another. With the absence of commercial toys, young children learned to play together and create their own entertainment, with more excitement than a whole day at the amusement park or video arcade. These home-spun adventures forged bonds with brothers, sisters, and family friends that remained strong for a lifetime.

When there were few jobs and no overtime, parents spent more time at home. It made a big difference in the pace of life. Whole families spent time together; grandparents often lived with the younger generation and passed on knowledge of the family roots. The interaction of grandparents and grandchildren formed such a strong love bond that it is hard for someone without this experience to understand the extent of influence the grandparents had on the grandchildren.

The one-room country school was not only an educational institution but an extension of family and was a center of community life. There was a sense of safety in knowing your neighbors, and in knowing that they would come to your aid if you needed them. These things characterized the rural people and days of the

Great Depression. Times were hard, but their spirits were strong. They did a lot more than survive—they built a legacy. With this in mind, I hope you enjoy this true account of growing up in rural Michigan during the 1930s.

Acknowledgments

A special acknowledgement to Sue Sprague, my wife of over fifty years, who aided in typing, proofreading, suggestions, editing, and encouragement.

To our daughters and their spouses, Karen and Leigh Burch, Pamela and Randy Wentzloff, and Nancy and Daryl Hamel. For their encouragement and proofreading. To our son and his spouse, Dr. Thomas and Carol Sprague, for the hours of technical assistance, printing of manuscripts, and proofing.

And to my brothers and sisters, Little Bill, Vera, Kenneth, Francis, and Joyce—without them and our collective adventures there would be no story.

Dedication

Dedicated to the memory of my grandparents, Libby and Bessie Sprague; my parents, William H. (Bill) and Thelma Sprague; to my brother and sister-in-law, William L. (Little Bill) and Doris Sprague, and to my sister and brother-in-law Vera and Donavon "Doc" Kaufman.

Memories

How long since we romped
on wood floors worn smooth?
We bumped and bruised and
mother would soothe.

Listened to Grandpa's tales
spun all night.
His pipe swirled smoke
rings in the lamp light.

Pestered, he gave grandkids his delight.

How long has it been?
Memories now still.

The Arrival

February 1931, winter began to show signs of slowing down. Snow still covered the ground, making it hard to do much outside. Dad and Grampa had been helping Andrew Kennedy and Hub Matthews prepare for maple-syrup time. They washed buckets, tapped trees, and cut wood for fuel to boil the sap into syrup. The chores finished and the evening meal behind them, the two men had retired to the dinning room to sit in front of the wood-burning stove. An evening of checkers was about to begin.

The checkerboard was hand painted and one set of checkers was cut from an old broom handle, the other cut from a one-inch square stick. With the checkers spread out before them and the game well under way, the men were deep in thought. Grampa, sensing a defeat, deployed his favorite diversion. Leaning back in the old wooden rocking chair, he placed his feet on the homemade footstool, reached over, and picked up his pipe. Packing it full of Union Leader tobacco, he started puffing away.

"Ya know Bill, did I ever tell ya how we came to be in Michigan?" Dad had heard the story many a time, but he just pushed the checkerboard aside and listened. Grampa did tell a good story and always with a little different twist to hold your interest. Already Grampa had accomplished one thing: he got Dad's mind off the game. Now he stalled for time to figure out his next move.

"Well, ya know, when your Grampa Hugh got home after fightin' those Southerners he was a little restless…" Grampa continued.

Hugh Sherman did have an interesting past. Born in Bethlehem, New Hampshire, at an early age his family had moved to a farm near Shapleigh, Maine. He worked with his dad and brothers on the farm and in the logging industry until March 1865. Then at seventeen he lied about his age and enlisted in the army. He was assigned to Company D, 1st Battalion, Maine Infantry. He served as a drummer and rifleman. After the Civil War he returned to Shapleigh, married Emma Smith, and their son Jessie was born. Shortly thereafter, homestead land opened in the western frontier of Wisconsin and Minnesota. The timbers of Maine had all but been depleted and the hilly farm his dad was working hardly made a living for him, let alone his four sons. Hugh's restless spirit and the lure of free land led him to head west by way of Michigan. It was late in the year when he packed his family in a covered wagon, thinking they would make it to their friends in Michigan before real cold weather. The family would stay with them for the winter and continue west in the spring. Emma was certainly happy when they reached Kawkawlin, in Bay County Michigan, as the winter chill could be felt in the air and that old covered wagon had bumped and jostled them around long enough, its wooden wheels banging over those rutted roads.

During the winter Hugh heard about a forty-acre farm for sale just outside of town. After inspection it was decided they would purchase it and settle in Michigan. Emma was really pleased not to have to travel any further. There was work in the logging business in Bay County and along with farming they could make a good living. Spring came and they moved to the farm and settled in. Their second son, Libby, was born in 1876. Jessie and Libby had lots of good memories as they grew up on that farm.

Grampa, still struggling to find a way to win this checker game, leaned over and studied his predicament and puffed a couple more times on his pipe; the glow of the burning tobacco shone bright red in the dimly lit room. The soft flicker of the flames from the fire in the heating stove shone through the isinglass door front, and the radiating heat swirled the pipe smoke upward to the ceiling.

Leaning back in the rocking chair and blowing a couple smoke rings toward the ceiling, Grampa continued. "I remember once when Jessie and I were left home alone. Jessie said it would be a good time to do something about those old dogs down the road that kept chasing the horses and had bitten nearly everyone in the area whenever they had gone by that house. He got down Dad's old army pistol, put that black powder in all six holes in the cylinder, and then put in the lead balls and covered them all with lard. He put the caps on and we were ready."

"We hooked the horses to the buggy and started down the road. Sure enough those dogs came out to greet us. We just kept the horses running 'til we were past the house and behind the trees that lined the roadway. Then Jessie pulled that old six-shooter from his belt. When the first dog was right by the front wheel, bang, a puff of smoke, and that dog just laid out in the road.

"Next one got close to the rear hooves of one of the horses, another puff of smoke and a yelp and that dog ran to the side of the road and rolled into the ditch." We just slowed the horses and waited for that third dog to catch up, then another bang and that dog said, 'twasn't I' and ran off. Jessie said that should take care of the problem, so we turned that old wagon around and headed home.

"Ya know there was a lot of talk about who killed those dogs. No one ever found out, and no one was sorry either. Everybody had trouble keeping their horses under control when they went that way to town."

"Well ya know, Dad, we better finish this game." Dad remarked, "I think I have you just where I want you."

Grampa looked down at the board, studied a while, and made his move. Dad was surprised to see he was in deep trouble. There was only one move he could make. Smiling, Grampa picked up his checker, and click-click, his checker tapped the board. He had double jumped, taking Dad's only king.

Now it was Dad who needed the time out. Well, he thought, the old pipe trick worked for Grampa. So he reached for his own pipe and took a couple draws. He was puzzled how to move.

"Getting a little chilly in here don't ya think?" Dad remarked.

He got up, opened the door of the stove, and stirred the embers in the fire pot with the poker. Throwing in a couple pieces of wood and opening the draft, he soon got the fire roaring. The metal of the stove snapped as it heated up.

"The wind is sure howling out there, takes the heat right out of the house," Dad said.

"Ya, I heard the women stoke up the kitchen range a few minutes ago. Can't figure out how those two can see to crochet and knit with just that oil lamp on the table between them," Grampa came back.

"What I marvel at, is how they can do it and chatter

as fast as they do," Dad said.

"Don't know, just glad they can sew. Grandma's old Singer machine is going good yet; don't know what we'd do without it." Grampa continued, "Your mother said she has to get her wool socks and mittens done this winter or it's going to be a skinny Christmas next December. Says she doesn't have time when spring gets here and the gardening and canning start."

"If this depression doesn't end soon it will be a skinny Christmas for sure, don't hardly have enough money for the rent let alone Christmas," Dad answered.

All this time Dad had been thinking about his next move. He had it. One slide of a checker and Grampa was on the defense again.

"Now Bill," Grampa leaned back again with pipe in hand, "When I was about your age, must have been about the turn of the century, that old wanderlust that your Grampa had bit me, and I took off for Kansas. I was going to work on one of those there traveling threshing crews; you know where they move along as the grain ripened until winter set in. By then you'd worked all the way to North Dakota. Well I didn't have any money. I just put everything I owned in an old flour sack, headed for Saginaw, and jumped the first freight train going west. On the way I worked at what ever I could find so as to have a little money to eat. There was always someone that needed something done. I was pretty handy and could fix most anything, and if I couldn't I just bluffed my way through. I'd be long gone before anyone found out I didn't know what I was doing, but I always made sure things were working before I left.

"Well I finally got to Kansas and started threshing. The pay wasn't good, and the work was seven days a week, hard, dirty, and hot. I figured the adventure was worth it.

"What I learned in the west changed my thinking. I found that even though I thought I could handle myself, there was always someone bigger and stronger. Fact was most of these men were tough, and didn't care about their family, if they even had one. They drank every night and loved to fight. Now you know I'm not beyond a little nip now and then myself, but every night, that's not for me. Well maybe it was 'cause I just didn't have the money for it. I could hold my own in a fair fight too, but out there it might be two or three against one. I didn't want any part of that, so I just sorted out a couple guys like myself and we just kept quiet and stuck together. In a way I was glad when the harvest was over, but I sure did like it out there and had really wanted to go onto California. I didn't make enough to do that so I went back to Kawkawlin. Got back there and didn't have any more money than when I started."

In 1902 Libby met and married Bessie Gorley, an Indian girl, ten years younger than him. Bessie had a young daughter, Vera Pearl. Bessie's mother had died giving birth to her and her twin sister Jessie. Jessie didn't live long after birth. Gramma Bessie's father, Edward, left her to be raised by a woman who worked as a cook in the logging camps. Bessie went to the camps with her, which was a pretty poor environment to grow up in.

"You know Bill," Grampa went on, "we're proud of you, Ike, Ruben, Lester, and Vera. Bill, I tried to provide for you guys. Your mother helped by working in the homes of neighbors; she took in washings and hired out as a midwife. She even delivered Helen, who is living with you now.

"Working in the coal mines near Bay City sure got to my back. Working in a crouch, I had to lift that heavy coal all day. That's why I went into the factories, but they were just sweatshops. Didn't pay well, and we had to work up to fourteen hours a day. We lived in a lot of places. The big downfall for you was when we moved next to the Miles family."

Dad just grinned. "Oh I kinda liked that Thelma Miles right from the beginning."

Thelma was the oldest daughter of Harry and Mary Miles. Her father was a heavy drinker and abusive to the family. He divorced Gramma when Mother was about twelve years of age. Gramma Mary had to go to work to provide for the family and Mother was saddled with caring for four younger siblings. Gramma Mary just couldn't make enough money to support her family, so Mother quit school at the end of the eighth grade and waited tables in a restaurant to help Gramma provide.

Later she worked summers with Dad weeding sugar beets and then in the fall topping the beets. One farmer didn't want to pay Mother the regular rate per row because he was afraid her four foot seven inches just wasn't large enough for her to keep up. What size has to do with how much you get paid per row no one knows, it just seems a way of getting cheap labor. He finally consented to pay her the same. Dad just made sure to work beside her. That way he could reach over and help her weed if she was getting behind. It wasn't long and the two were romancing, and married in August of '26.

The next two years were hard. They worked as migrant farm hands. Started in the thumb area with sugar beets and celery, and then headed north to pick wild huckleberries, blackberries, and sweet and sour cherries in the orchards near Traverse City. Later summer found them along the Lake Michigan shore picking peaches, then apples in the fall. During the winter months they did odd jobs in the Bay area. When a farmer near Constantine offered Dad a full-time job, he jumped at it. The pay wasn't much but he furnished milk, eggs, meat, and a house in addition to the cash. Just in time too—Little Bill, their first child, was about to be born.

"Dad I sure remember that August of '27," Bill remarked, twisting his head to one side. "We lived on that tenant farm for over a year. Then I started working in the foundry at the Viking Corporation in Hastings. That move to Hastings was hard. We didn't have a way to haul our belongings. Boy, things happened pretty fast. First the move, then the stock market collapsed and Vera was born in December. Now here we are two years later; no money, little work, and struggling to make ends meet.

"Dad, I don't think either one of us wants to finish this game, it looks like a draw to me, how about you?"

"Well I know I can beat you, but to let you save face, I'll let you call it a draw," Grampa came back.

The checkers were soon put away and the fire fixed for the night.

"Goodnight, see you in the morning. Thelma, you coming to bed?" Dad called out.

The Early Years

It was the summer of 1931. Dad and Mother were struggling to make ends meet. To provide better for the family, they had moved into a three-bedroom house, two miles east of town. In addition to the house there was a large hip-roof barn, chicken coop, corncrib, and ample room for a large garden. Bordering all this on the east were several apple trees. They purchased a Jersey cow named Bessie, a large flock of Plymouth Rock chickens, a couple pigs, and several geese. The milk, eggs, meat, and garden produce gave them an assurance that there would be no shortage of food to fill the canning jars and pickling crocks.

Mother and Dad sensed a moral obligation to our extended family, so they opened our home to Dad's parents and to Mother's younger sister, thirteen-year-old Helen Miles. With these additions the house was filled to capacity. Before the decade of the thirties passed many more family members stayed with us. Some stayed for a short time, others stayed for several months.

The morning of July 27, 1931 started like any other hot and humid summer day in south-central Michigan. As the morning progressed, though, it became clear that this was not to be an ordinary day.

Mother sat sipping a cup of green tea at the just-cleared breakfast table. Gramma stood at the crude wooden counter washing dishes in the old round porcelain dishpan, then placed them in the cast-iron sink. She reached over with a large dipper, scooped hot water from the built-in reservoir of the wood-burning cook stove, and poured it over the dishes to rinse them.

"Hot enough outdoors without having this stove going today," Gramma remarked.

Suddenly Mother got a stern look on her face and clinched her fist. Everything was quiet for a while, and then she relaxed.

"A little harder this time?" asked Gramma.

"A little and lasted longer too," said Mother.

You could see Gramma's pace pick up as she hurried to finish the dishes. Reaching to the other end of the counter, she picked up the half-full pail of water and poured it into the reservoir. "Helen, would you get a bucket of water, seems we're going to need it before this day is over."

Taking the pail, Helen headed for the hand pump about a hundred feet north from the house. Returning, she saw Little Bill riding his wild bronco—a stick he had straddled—shouting, "Come on Vera, hurry up." He raced into the kitchen and around the homemade wooden plank table. Lagging far behind came little eighteen-month-old Vera as fast as she could toddle. She was jumping and yelling, trying to imitate little Bill's actions.

"Helen, you'll have to keep the children out of the kitchen, Gramma has too many things to get done today to have them under my feet." She turned to the little ones, "Now, out of here!" The wild bronco wheeled and carried little Bill back into the living room as Helen picked up Vera and off they scurried.

That morning, Dad and Grampa Libby had gone to help the neighbor get ready for wheat harvest, unaware of what was in store when they returned for lunch. As the two men walked up the long sandy driveway, Gramma hurried to meet them.

"Bill it's time to get the doctor! Thelma's been in labor all morning, and the pains are getting close together and hard. I thought you would never get here!" Gramma said.

Without hesitation Dad jumped into the old Chevy touring car and drove off down the road, sending dust flying. It was just two miles to town, but what if Doc Adroinie wasn't there? He made so many house calls; there would be no way to find him.

Meanwhile the feverish pace continued in the kitchen as Gramma scurried about. She got towels and a clean

13

blanket and took them to the bedroom, then she grabbed a large white pan for water and took it to the bedroom.

"There, I think that's all we're going to need except the hot water," she said as she turned and tried to comfort Mother. The birthing process was nothing new for Gramma; she had given birth to five children of her own and worked as a midwife in Bay City and Flint. She had helped deliver some of Mother's siblings.

"Bill and the doctor will be here soon. Would you like to go in and lie down?" Gramma put another piece of wood in the kitchen range, "Got to get this water hot."

"No, I'm going to stay up as long as I can. Goin' in will be bad enough when I have to." Mother replied as she grasped her stomach and held her breath. Soon she relaxed. "That was a rough one, I hope they hurry."

A short time later they heard the sound of two cars coming up the drive. Dad had returned with the doctor.

"How's everything?" he asked as he burst into the kitchen.

"She's in bed now. I'm glad you weren't any later."

Dr. Adroinie came in with his black bag and was escorted directly to the bedroom. The door closed and the wait began.

Dad and Grampa tried to make small talk and attempted to help Helen contain the two little ones. Foremost on their minds was what was going on behind the closed door. Dad and Grampa nervously paced around the room, reassuring each other all was going well with Mother. Little Bill and Vera, oblivious to the happenings, entertained themselves first with dolls, then with trucks, and then back to the wild bronco.

Dad's mind kept wandering to what-ifs. What if there are complications, what if the child dies, what if Thelma dies? The suspense was overwhelming. He tried to force himself not to think that way. He turned his thoughts to the extra mouth to feed. We hardly made it now, he thought, seven people to feed already. My job isn't that stable, and I only work one or two days a week. Without that I couldn't even pay the rent. Good thing I'm working for the neighbors. No money there but it gives us feed for the livestock and wheat for flour. I know Grampa works whenever work is available and Gramma sure does her share of the house work. I don't even know where I'm going to get the money to pay Doc.

The high suspense made the seconds drag. Time just seemed to stop; would the baby ever come? Then it was over, my first cry was heard. Gramma came out of the bedroom. "It's a boy, everything's okay!"

Dad slipped into the bedroom and up to the bed where Mother lay holding me. He leaned over, hugged Mother, and held her for a moment. Kissing her on the forehead, he sat down on the edge of the bed. No words were necessary; the proud smile on his face told it all.

"You okay?"

Mother nodded and smiled, "He's so healthy." She had turned the attention to the new life wrapped in a flannel blanket on the pillow next to her. Dad lifted my hand with his callused, leathery finger.

"Sure is little," he remarked, then again turned back to Mother making her as comfortable as possible. Fatigue was causing her eyes to become heavy. "Better get some rest while this little guy's asleep. It's getting late, so I better milk the cow before she thinks I've deserted her."

Gramma was already busy with the evening meal as Dad grabbed the milk pail from the shelf over the sink on his way through the kitchen. "Be about an hour," he called back as he bounced out the door and down the steps to the barn.

Dad returned from the chores of milking, feeding the livestock, and gathering the eggs. There was a new bucket of milk to strain and a basket of eggs to wash before they were stored in the icebox. The milk was poured through a cloth stretched over a pail to strain out anything that could have fallen in the milk. It was then put into several two-quart glass jars for storage in the cistern outside. (A cistern is nothing more then a hole dug about six feet deep in the hard red-clay earth, lined with brick or stone, and covered to keep it clean.) It would hold large volumes of cold soft rainwater to be used for cooling foods and for washing clothes. Perishable foods were placed on a platform made of wood, and then lowered by rope into the water.

It had been a long hard day for Gramma; the evening meal was over and the dishes done. Little Bill and Vera were fast asleep. Helen had long since retired to bed. Dad and Grampa were in the living room, deep in thought over a checker game. Now it was Gramma's time as she sat at the kitchen table in the soft flickering light of the oil lamp, the teapot steaming near her. With pencil in hand, she started a letter to Gramma Mary, my maternal grandmother, telling her about her new grandson. Finishing, she blew out the oil lamp, walked into the dinning room, and up the open stairway that led to her bedroom. Thoughts of the next day were already starting to go through her mind. Grampa followed. The exhausted family had now all retired for the night. Tomorrow would bring its own triumphs and disappointments, but for now contentment filled the air.

"It's been a good day," Gramma murmured as she drifted off to sleep.

The summer progressed and the garden started to yield its bounty. The Depression was deepening. Dad's work in town was now only a few hours a week. Fieldwork for the farmers was all bartered. A day's work might net a small pig; a week's work might bring a calf or hay, whatever the farmer could spare—often a farmer could give nothing. Folks still willingly helped each other without compensation of any kind. It was the only way they could survive, and survive they did.

Summer was soon over and Helen was to enter the eighth grade at the one-room Fisher school. Mother, trying her best to be a good replacement mother for Helen, told her she could have a Halloween party and to invite all her friends from school. Helen excitedly did just that.

Mother and Gramma worked hard and long making cupcakes and other treats. They made decorations from anything they could find. The big day arrived, but something was wrong! The crowd just kept growing; it seemed the whole neighborhood was showing up. Frantically, Mother wondered how to make the treats go around!

"Bessie, what are we going to do?" Mother asked. "We just don't have enough for all these people!"

"Don't know, we'll just have to make it go as far as we can," replied Gramma.

Meanwhile the men, being entertained by Grampa and Dad, were happily and noisily carrying on in the living room. The hard cider they served from the barrel in the basement was doing its job. All the time the noisy children were running in and out of the house having a great time.

More people kept strolling up the driveway. Mother was just in a panic until she saw a couple of the ladies carrying plates of cookies and cupcakes. "Oh am I ever glad to see you two. I never expected so many people to show, I didn't make enough of anything."

"We thought you might need a little help. Where should we put this stuff?" said one of the women.

"Just on the table where ever you can find room. Boy you sure saved the day," Mother answered. With the party behind them and all back to normal, Mother asked Helen whom she had invited.

"Oh, I just said at school it was for everyone," Helen answered.

"Well everything worked out okay, I did have a good time visiting with the women, and the men certainly enjoyed that hard cider!"

There was little in the way of material possessions for the average family of the Fisher school community. The big thing going for them was the willingness to help one another and share what they had. Rural people needed each other, and they counted on one another to help in farming and daily activities. In the years to come, that spirit was to be tested to a far greater degree than anyone could have realized. The depression of the 30s brought about bankruptcy and suicides. Homes were lost and families were forced into the streets. In the large cities soup lines were set up to feed the destitute. But through it all, rural communities like ours pulled together and survived.

Family Capers

Autumn was in its entire splendor! The sun was glistening on trees dressed in their fall hues of reds and yellows. All summer the large garden had produced vegetables: radishes, onions, green beans, cucumbers, summer squash, and early potatoes. Wild and tame blackberries and raspberries had been picked and preserved. Now in the fall large quantities of tomatoes, winter squash, sweet corn, white beans, and cabbages were harvested. The apples, pears, and peaches were ripening. A time of plenty but a time of hard work as well.

The men usually gathered the produce. Potatoes, apples, and squash were stored in the cool, dry basement. The women canned everything else. A typical fall would find up to four hundred quarts of canned foods lining the shelves. Meat from the butchered pigs and cows were canned, smoked, or salted as there was no electricity for refrigeration

Fall also brought some money from the sale of pelts

of muskrat, raccoon, weasel, opossum, mink, and skunk. The raccoon also made good table fare. The hunting of small game such as rabbit, pheasant, and squirrel added fresh meat. This was not an unfamiliar lifestyle for Dad. Grampa had taught him and his three brothers the art of hunting and trapping. As children they had always fished, skills that were now serving Dad well.

One Sunday morning in the early winter, Grampa Miles, Mother's father, came to hunt rabbits. Pulling into the driveway and parking, he was met by Dad and Grampa Sprague. Guns in hand, they were ready for a day in the field. Retrieving his gun from the back seat, Grampa Miles loaded it as the three started for the field.

"All set. Why don't we walk the fence row north past the barn?" Dad remarked. "Always lots of tracks there and usually a rabbit or two."

"I'll get the first one." Grampa Miles said.

"Think you're fast enough now days to get a shot off before the rabbit gets out of sight?" shot back Grampa Sprague.

"You two old guys quit your hassling, I'm not sure either of you could hit one if you did get a shot, so I'll show ya how it's done!"

Dad climbed the fence. The three started walking north. Bang, a shot rang out! Grampa Sprague yelled as he strutted up to the rabbit, "I guest you guys are all talk." Reaching down and picking it up he found, to his amazement, the rabbit was caught in one of Dad's traps. Too late, both of the others had seen the trap dangling from the rabbit's front feet. There was silence. The look on Grampa's face told it all. He knew he was in trouble! It wasn't going to go away easily or soon!

"Ha! Ha! Ha!" rang out from the two bystanders as they doubled up with laughter. Catching their breath long enough to slap their thighs, they started all over again. Tears ran down their cheeks as they strolled up to Grampa Sprague, busily trying to get the trap off.

"Dad, this was supposed to be a fair chase. Why didn't you let him out of the trap first?" Dad remarked.

"One thing for sure, if you had missed him you could get another shot." Grampa Miles teased.

The good-natured kidding continued for a while. Finally Grampa composed himself. "At least I have a rabbit."

The hunt was to last most of the morning, one of many hunts the three would engage in over the next few years. Returning, the men cleaned and washed the game. The meat was then put in salt water to leach out the blood.

Grampa Miles went to his car. "Got something to warm us up." He took a quart jar from the back seat. "This is a little of my famous elderberry wine." He held it high as he started for the house.

Grampa Sprague perked right up, "I think I can do with a little warming."

Both grampas sat at the table as Dad took three glasses from the cupboard.

"Think these will hold enough to get you warm?" asked Dad.

Grampa Sprague smacked his lips as he took a sip, remarking, "Boy, this will light up my nose. It's powerful!"

"Dad that nose of yours gives you away," Dad shot back.

"Ya, it got me into trouble more than once. Every time I had a little nip, Bessie could always tell. It would turn as red as a hot coal."

"Well Dad, it's beginning to look like a beacon already," Dad said.

That evening Gramma and Mother stoked up the old wood-burning cook stove, and before long the smell of fresh-baked biscuits and frying rabbit filled the air. Later as they sat enjoying the meal, all realized this had cost them very little—the good Lord had provided. Activities such as hunting, fishing, and Mother's favorite, ice skating, were a welcome relief from the dreary conditions of the worsening depression. Evenings were spent playing cards, checkers, reading, and socializing with neighbors.

Winter had now lost some of its sting; spring was coming. Aunt Helen would soon be out of school, and sometime in the summer she would be returning home to her own mother in Lansing. She had mixed emotions about this. The year had been a good one. She and Mother had grown close, a closeness that would last the rest of their lives, as would her admiration and appreciation for Dad.

In February of 1933 my brother Kenneth was born; as we grew it brought about major changes in Mother and Dad's lives. Four children under six years of age put a tremendous physical burden on Mother, and the added expense stretched the already strapped financial budget even further.

One evening Dad and Mother were reminiscing about an event that still brought horror to their minds. A container of formaldehyde had sat on the front porch. It was poisonous and was used to treat seeds for insects before planting. Mother walked out of the kitchen door and was astonished to see that somehow three-year-old Little Bill had removed the cap and placed the bottle to his lips.

"Don't drink that!" she screamed jerking it from his hands. "Bill, help me! Billy drank formaldehyde!"

Not knowing how much he consumed, if any, they picked him up and hurried off to the doctor. Fortunately they had caught him in time; he had ingested none.

As the children grew, Little Bill took on the role of big brother. Sometimes this was good; he often kept the smaller ones from harm. But all too often, he conned us younger ones into doing things for him. Still all in all we played well together and became very clannish and protective of one another. Winter or summer, weather permitting, we were outside. Vera was fast becoming a tomboy keeping up with the boys very well. Mother began worrying whether she would ever become a lady.

One afternoon on a warm summer day, while Mother was busy in the kitchen, she was surprised to hear a car door close. It was much too early for Dad to be home. Wiping her hands on her apron she walked to the door just in time to see a Watkins salesman returning to his car and backing out of the driveway. Strange action she thought, looking down she noticed the problem. Sitting on the cast-aluminum cooker she had received as a Christmas present sat eighteen-month-old Kenneth. He was using it for a toilet.

"My cooker!" she yelled. It was too late; Ken had finished his job. With heaviness in her heart, Mother walked the path to the outhouse and dumped the contents. The cooker just changed its role from cookware to dog dish. So were the daily occurrences with four active children. In July, Aunt Helen returned for a short stay.

One evening while she was there, Gramma and Grampa came down from their room carrying a small box. "We've decided to give these things to Tom. When he gets older we want him to have them, and to keep them in the family." Opening the box they showed three items that Great Grampa Sprague had brought home from the Civil war: a picture of his wife's father (our great, great Grampa Smith, who had been a cook for

General Grant), a salesman's sample bale of cotton, and a newspaper reporting the execution of the accomplices of John Wilkes Booth.

Taking them Mother replied, "I'll take good care of them for Tom." The picture has been lost over the years. The other two items remain in the family today.

The Goose Chase

Vera was now four years old and, like the rest of the children, enjoyed being outdoors when the sun shone. All summer she had persisted in chasing the chickens and geese. Mother would say, "Vera, quit chasing the chickens."

"But I'm not chasing them, I'm following them!" Vera would reply.

One old gander did not take kindly to being chased. Each time Vera went outside he would peck at the seat of her pants. Mother did her best to protect Vera, to no avail. The goose would always win, and Vera would run to the house in tears. Two things would be accomplished that November: Vera would no longer be chased, and a grand Thanksgiving feast would center around her tormentor.

Mother, six months pregnant with Francis (born November 2, 1934), was trying to prepare for the coming school year. It was a challenge without money. People learned to improvise in hard times, and Mother mastered the art. She made dresses for Vera using old clothes and leftover scraps from other sewing projects. When the sewing scraps ran out, she finished Vera's wardrobe by cutting up printed flour sacks. Milling companies saw an opportunity in the depression market, and packaged flour in cloth bags printed in floral patterns and other designs. Mother was a good seamstress, and had an eye for fashion. This ensured a nice wardrobe for Vera and herself.

The school year started. Little Bill was now a seasoned pro, a second grader. Vera started in the first grade—there was no kindergarten in those days. Each morning little Bill would take her hand, "Come on Vera, we've got to hurry—the neighbor kids are coming." Skipping down the driveway they would join other neighborhood children on their way to school. Vera wasn't five until December, and at this age was very apprehensive. Arriving the first morning she started crying. The teacher tried to comfort her without success. Finally, in desperation, she picked her up, gave her one soft swat on the seat, and sat her down.

"Now young lady you have something to cry about."

Suddenly, Vera adjusted to school, with no more crying.

At home for the next two or three weeks Little Bill would quiz Vera about his schoolwork. Of course she didn't know the answers. He would look at her and shake his head. He could not figure out why she didn't know everything he did.

"She sure is dumb," Little Bill would say. No amount of explaining could convince him that Vera was younger and would learn as she advanced. To him she was just a dumb sister.

In early September Mother received a letter from her sister Pearl, saying they planned to come the following Saturday and stay overnight. They would return to Lansing on Sunday. Pearl's husband, Ernie Wilson, was not a country man. In fact, he was quite apprehensive of staying overnight in "the wilderness." Ernie and Pearl had five children too, about the same age as us kids. When we learned our city cousins were coming we were very excited.

Dad, knowing of Ernie's fears, was not willing to let the opportunity pass. He set about getting an old shirt, pants, and a white sheet. When he told the children what he was going to do he had eager assistants to stuff the clothes with hay. Off to the barn we went laughing and buzzing about the trick we were going to pull on Uncle Ernie.

"First, let me tie the bottom of the legs with string so you kids can stuff them full with hay," instructed Dad.

With the pants stuffed, the shirt was pinned to the pants, and it was stuffed too. Lastly, a sheet was fashioned to form a head with the excess material flowing loosely down over the ghostly body. Perfect, the dummy was complete!

We borrowed a rope from Mother's cloth line and tied it high in the tree. Then we stretched it down to the top of the window in the bedroom where Pearl and Ernie would sleep. A coat hanger attached the dummy to the rope. Great! Now all that was left to do was tie another rope to the dummy and up to the second-story window. A test was made; everything worked perfectly! By pulling on the rope from the second story the dummy slid toward the house bouncing and swinging as it went. A slight breeze fluttered the sheet. Sliding down the rope, it came directly to the bedroom window. The trick was now set.

"Okay, let's get this guy back into the tree so no one will see it."

"How are we going to wake up Ernie in the middle of the night?" asked Mother.

"I have that figured out. We'll tie a bolt to a string, and lower it down from the upstairs bedroom window. Then, we'll swing it against the window of the bedroom they're in." This was soon finished, and we were ready.

"Don't tell anyone about this when Uncle Ernie gets here," we were cautioned.

Anxiously we awaited their arrival—four o'clock, then six o'clock, but still no Wilsons. Now darkness was setting in, and reality sat in as well. The Wilsons were not coming. Everyone had worked so hard to get things perfect. But as the old quote goes, "Anticipation is greater then realization." The joke was on us.

Late fall, the canning was finished, butchering done, the apples, potatoes, and the squash in the basement. Now time to prepare for the great feast, Thanksgiving. Dad was up early, delighted in the approaching execution of the goose that had been almost devious in stalking Vera, the apple of his eye. The time was now! Dad set the block of wood just right so it would not tip or rock. He checked the axe for sharpness and went off to find Mr. Goose. With poultry hook in hand, he started the stalk.

The gander, sensing his peril, ran from one part of the yard to another; he was always just out of reach. Around the apple trees, to the barn and back, and through the heavy brushed fencerow, Dad was always in hot pursuit. Dad lunged with the hook, trying to catch a leg in the wire end. Just missed, the goose was off again. Finally in a last exhausted dive the goose's leg was hooked. Mr. Goose, with wings flopping and honking at full volume, made a last desperate attempt at his freedom.

Now if you think it was all over for the goose, you have never engaged a twenty-pound half-wild barnyard gander. Realizing his plight, the bird turned on Dad. With wings arched and beak snapping he stretched out his neck and attacked. Dad grabbed for the neck. He had the critter, only to discover the real battle had just begun. Flapping and kicking the goose proceeded to batter and bruise Dad, but somehow he held on. The two combatants were poised to battle until the end. Dad was determined to win at any cost, so as not to be defeated by a goose. Mr. Goose, on the other hand, was fighting for his life. Fatigue took its toll on man and bird. With a last ditch effort, Dad finally contained first the wings and then the feet. The bird was subdued, and taken to the chopping block!

With one arm around the body to hold the wings, and the other hand holding the neck, Dad suddenly realized he had a problem. If he let go of the neck to pick up the axe, he would be pecked bloody. If he let go of the wings, he would get beaten black-and-blue. Dad was troubled over the predicament. Ah, the perfect solution! He put the goose's head on the chopping block, holding it with his foot. With the head pinned by his foot, he reached for the axe. It was too far away! Wearily, he grabbed the neck again and squeezed the goose's head under his arm. This freed an elbow and a hand just enough to retrieve the axe. Once again, the goose's head was pinned to the block with a foot as Dad balanced on the other. Now, he finally had a whole arm free for the axe. But from this awkward position, it was next to impossible to swing. Well, there would be only one chance! He took a clumsy but well-aimed swing. Dad couldn't keep his balance, but on the way down, the goose lost its head. The battle was over! Dad, the axe, and the goose's head and body went in four different directions. Ah the sweet taste of victory! Dad took just a minute to catch his breath and the glory of triumph; he had won!

Meanwhile Mother built a fire in the wood-burning range to heat water. The goose was brought into the kitchen, dipped in the hot water to loosen the feathers, and placed on the work area. Together she and Dad started plucking feathers.

With perspiration still running down his brow, Dad showed her the bruises on his arm and confessed, "For a while I wasn't sure who was going to win."

"Now that the goose is oven-ready, I'll make the bread stuffing and get this guy ready to cook all night," Mom said.

The kitchen had been abuzz all day with activity. Gramma and Mother had baked pies and a chocolate cake, peeled potatoes, and prepared all sorts of Thanksgiving treats. The aroma of the grand feast permeated the house. The goose, baking at a slow simmer, added another delicious aroma, heightening the anticipation of the meal. Preparations continued late into the evening. Finally Dad and Mother were ready for bed.

"I sure showed that gander whose boss," Dad said.

"Sure did," Mother chuckled, as she drifted off to sleep.

Dad had several opportunities to glory in his victory over the goose as he stoked the wood fire to keep the goose cooking slowly all night. Mother was up early Thanksgiving morning, adding fresh wood and opening the draft to start the flames blazing high. The women prepared breakfast while the men did the farm chores.

With the outside farm chores finished, the storage box filled with dry split wood for the kitchen, and the wood pile behind the space heater in the dinning room replenished, the adults sat down to breakfast. They enjoyed a break before the children were up.

Thanksgiving dinner was always later than regular lunch to allow for family activities, and to give travel time for anyone who might be coming. It was a great time for relatives to get together and spin tales of family no longer with them. Soon the long awaited words were heard: "Dinner's ready." We all sat down, along with Grampa Miles who had joined us for the day, to a meal that was duplicated only at Christmas.

After finishing the sumptuous feast, Dad slid his chair back, "Great meal, women! One thing's for sure, I fixed that old gander so he will never chase Vera again, but he did put up a real battle."

Grampa Goes
to the Hospital

In 1936 the Depression was showing signs of lessening. Dad and Grampa were getting more work for cash, and the farmers had a good maple sugar year. The spring's field work was off to a good start! Homer Becker had been working the ground almost all winter; now he was tilling the field next to the house. All of us kids were fascinated as we watched the large draft horses strain into the traces pulling the field drag that prepared the soil for planting. I walked out into the field to get a better look at the big steeds as they trudged along. Turning the corner at the end of the field and starting toward me, the animals again leaned into their collars. As they came close Homer pulled on the reins and stopped.

"Like to ride?" Homer asked.

I just stood there for a while. "YES!" I yelled back.

Homer picked me up and placed me on the back of one of those massive animals. "Just hold on here," he instructed as he placed my hands on the shiny brass balls atop the hames.

When the horses started, I felt the muscles flex beneath my legs as they pulled ahead. I was afraid at first but soon my thoughts started running wild. I was on some big adventure out in some far-off land! I pictured myself on the back of an elephant. That all stopped as we made our way around the field to the house. Back home again, Homer helped me to the ground.

"Thanks!" I ran for the house to tell Mother. "Ma, it was so fun! I rode on the horse! It's a long ways up in the air on top of him! He's so big! Boy are they strong!"

"Well did you thank him?" asked Mother.

"Ya," I replied.

"I don't think you should bother Mr. Becker any more," Mother said.

"I won't, I'll just go watch him," I answered.

"Stay on the edge of the field," she cautioned as I ran back.

People of the area were beginning to make long-overdue repairs as money was a little easier to come by. Still, the economy had a long way to go before things would be back to normal. Grampa's odd jobs, along with Gramma's paper hanging, were bringing in enough steady money for them to rent a house in Hastings. They also received a small monthly check from the government. It was a deduction from the wages of their sons, Ruben and Lester, who were serving in the Civilian Conservation Corps.

There wasn't any more room in the house when Gramma and Grampa moved into town. My Uncle Roy Miles and his wife and daughter, Marie, moved in. Uncle Roy, Mother's oldest brother, was out of work. No one believed it would be long before another job would come along. Marie was elated with the new experience of living in the country, and she now had lots of cousins to play with. Vera was happy too! There was another girl in the house so she wouldn't have to play with just boys.

The family was there longer than expected. It was late summer before Uncle Roy found work and returned to Lansing. The summer went well as the two families blended together. Marie learned all about frogs, toads, and mud puddles through first-hand experience, and quite often by a lot of trickery. My brothers and I delighted in getting Marie to try something we knew would get her in trouble. Vera tried to warn her, but usually to no avail.

While the children played, a worry dominated the minds and time of the adults that year. Grampa Sprague had stomach problems in the past, but this was different. The situation had become very serious, and he was hospitalized. After several days of treatment, his condition only worsened. The prognosis was bleak; his gall bladder was poisoning his body. There could be no treatment for him in Hastings. Dr. Adroinie contacted the University of Michigan Medical Center to see if they would be willing to do an experimental operation—the removal of his gall bladder. The family was informed that without the surgery Grampa would die. Word soon came back that the University would accept him. When Grampa was told about the operation and its implications, he had one request; he wanted to see me before he left. Hospital policy however would not allow visitors under twelve years of age. Special permission was granted, so Mother and Dad drove home to get me.

Gramma and Grampa had a love for all their grandchildren, but a great bond had taken place between them and me. This was easy to understand. I was the first grandchild Gramma had helped deliver, and she had helped care for me ever since. This care had released Mother from much work, but the bond between my grandparents and me was hard for Mother to handle. She felt she had lost me to them.

I looked with great amazement as we entered the hospital. Here was a building larger then anything I had ever seen. I gazed at everything as we walked the long halls and up the stairs to the third floor that housed critical-care patients. I was overwhelmed by all the hustle and bustle of the staff scurrying about their business. With those unusual smells, and all the sick people lying about, I was afraid but felt safe with Mother and Dad at my side. Soon I would see Grampa, but I didn't know what to expect.

A nurse escorted us to Grampa. Walking into the

room I looked at my Grampa lying pale and motionless on the bed. "You have a special visitor Libby." Turning to leave she cautioned, "Don't stay too long."

Mother took me by the hand. I reluctantly went to the bed. All kinds of emotions were going through my young mind. Fear, because I didn't know what was happening. I couldn't understanding why my Grampa was not the vibrant person he had always been. All of us children had memories of going up the stairs, from the time we were so small we had to crawl, and being welcomed into that small room by beloved and active grandparents.

Grampa opened his eyes and reached to place his arm around my back. Gripping my shoulder he said, "Sure am glad you came."

Fear and lack of understanding kept me from saying much, but talk was not necessary; I was with my Grandpa. After a short visit we had to leave. The next morning Dad's brother, Uncle Ruben, took Grampa to Ann Arbor. No one could stay with him and news about his condition was slow getting to the family. After an agonizing wait, a letter arrived. Grampa had come through the operation and was doing well. Though he was very weak, great relief settled over the entire family. At least one thing had gone right!

Grampa was still in the hospital when the sheriff's department forwarded a message that his father, Hugh Sherman Sprague, had died. Grampa Hugh had lived in

Kawkawlin since coming to Michigan. Under the advice of his doctor, Grampa was not told of his father's death; they feared that in his weakened condition the shock would be too much for him.

Some time later word was received that Grampa could come home. Dad, Mother, and Gramma left early in the morning for Ann Arbor. Gramma had given up their rented house in Hastings and returned to live with us in the country. Uncle Roy and Aunt Thelma had returned to Lansing as Uncle Roy had steady employment. Later that afternoon the old Chevy turned onto the dusty driveway. Grampa was exhausted, but happy to be home. My siblings and I could hardly contain our excitement. There was still the nagging question, what had happened to change Grampa? He had been an energetic and exciting man. Who was this tired, frail, old man who needed help to climb out of the car and get into the house? At sixty-three, he never completely recovered.

I sat in the rope swing hanging from a branch of the apple tree close to the driveway. All kinds of worried thoughts drifted through my mind about Grampa's condition. Swinging just enough to drag my feet in the dirt under the swing, my head drooped low; I was worried about Grampa and I was restless. I looked up and a desire to climb to the top of the tree came over me. It was no challenge; I had done it many times. With my mind more on Grampa than climbing, I climbed higher and higher.

Losing my grip, I slipped down the tree, coming to rest as my leg wedged between two branches of the tree. When I was unable to free myself I started yelling. No one heard me, so I started to panic. I yelled louder and louder and tears started to flow. The more I struggled the tighter my leg became lodged. A slight breeze swayed the branches. Each time the branch moved my leg was pinched tighter. I thought no one was ever going to hear, so I yelled louder! Finally, Mother heard my desperate calls. Running to the tree she climbed up to free my leg but she couldn't! Then Gramma arrived, climbed the tree, and sat on the outer branch to force the limbs apart. Mother jerked my leg free. I was one frightened and bruised little boy. I was lowered to the ground and carried to the house. I had learned my first lesson of common sense well. Nothing more needed to be said about the dangers of climbing. I would climb again, but hopefully would be more careful.

Time passed and Grampa regained some of his old spark. The stories that excited the children returned. The old man had not lost his ability to tantalize us. We sat for hours and listened as Grampa relived tales of the bygone days, adding just enough fiction to color the story and hold our young minds in suspense. Puffing on his pipe filled with Union Leader tobacco, he would sit back and blow smoke rings as the story unfolded to a very critical punch line. Then he'd stop and very deliberately refill and light his pipe before going on, while we sat spellbound. Times were back to normal; we had our good old Grampa back.

Pigs, Pigeons, and Chickens

The summer was going smoothly, Grampa was recovering nicely, and preparations for school were nearly complete. Most of the vegetables were canned and the daily routine was slowing. One afternoon when Mother was checking her canned goods, she discovered several quarts of pickles had spoiled. Not wanting to waste anything, she emptied the pickles into a bucket and carried the bucket to the barnyard. She dumped them into the hogs' feed trough. The two pigs came running and greedily consumed the pickles.

Dad would be home from work soon, so Mother started preparing the evening meal. She soon heard the unusually loud pig squeals. Somehow it didn't sound normal. Out of concern Mother removed her apron, placed it on the table, and started toward the barn. The squeals became erratic. She was sure something out of the ordinary was happening. Fear clutched her mind as she started running. Reaching the pigpen and, gazing over the old board fence, she was horror-struck. The pigs could no longer walk; instead they were leaning stiff-legged against the fence. Oink, oink, and then a squeal; something was terribly wrong. One pig was trying to walk and staggered to the center of the pen. It fell over. Lying on its side, it just lay there and squealed long and loud. Just then Dad drove into the driveway. Mother went running to meet him. With arms waving wildly to catch his attention, she sobbed loudly and made a tearful confession.

"Bill, Bill come quick! I've killed the pigs!"

Dad jumped from the car and dashed to the pigpen. He was thinking about a whole year's worth of meat lost. Where would the money come from to replace them? Even if we could replace the pigs, it would take six months before they would be ready to butcher. Grasping the top of the board fence, he anxiously peered over just in time to see one pig attempt to walk.

Staggering forward the pig managed to keep its feet under itself until it reached the fence. Falling against the fence, it dropped its head and started squealing wildly. The second pig in the center of the pen struggled to get his front feet under himself. He sat on his haunches, his front feet spread far apart for balance, swinging his head from side to side, and squealed with each motion.

"What'd you do to them?" Dad anxiously asked.

"I fed them pickles that were spoiled, but I didn't think it would kill them. They were okay at first. Then this started." The tears were flowing freely down Mother's cheeks.

The excitement beckoned the little ones. We gathered around the wooden fence. Peeking through the cracks, we could also see the antics. It was funny to watch. We were unaware of the seriousness of the ordeal so we just pointed at the pigs and laughed.

Dad put his arm around Mother. "Do you know what's wrong? They're drunk! Those pickles must have been fermented."

Mother relaxed a little, not knowing if she should believe him. "You sure? We can't afford to lose them."

"I'm sure. They'll be fine in the morning—just a little hung over," Dad reassured her.

After watching the pigs a while longer, we started for the house. Still laughing, the kids ran ahead. Dad put his arm around Mother as they too started for the house. "We'll check in a couple of hours. You'll see, they'll be sleeping it off. Good thing you didn't feed those pickles to the kids, we'd have had a real circus around here!"

All of us kids enjoyed going to the old hip-roof barn, north of the house. We would feed the pigs handfuls of grass or an ear of corn, and watch them consume whatever we fed them. We played in the hay or in the granary, which made a great playhouse. With all the time spent in the barn, Little Bill had developed a new talent. He could climb the inside framing of the barn to the window in the gable end about twenty-five feet above the hayloft floor. Now all sorts of adventure followed, most of it not very safe. Depending on the time of the year, the loft could be empty or full of hay.

One day as we played in the barn, several pigeons flew around. Vera pointed toward them and suggested, "Boy wouldn't it be nice if we could get one of those birds?"

"We can," Little Bill assured her. "I'll climb to the window, you guys scare them and when they fly out the window I'll grab one." The hayloft was about half full, so he went up the ladder to the top of the loose hay. He waded through to the end of the barn, and started the climb to the window. "This will be fun! When I get there start yelling to scare the pigeons and when I catch one I'll jump down."

Up the framing he went, first reaching and grabbing the horizontal beams with his hand and then pulling himself up. Beam after beam, soon he was in position just below the window. To the rest of us, Little Bill looked like a speck; he was so far above us. "Okay, I'm ready," Little Bill yelled. "Start scaring 'em."

Vera and I threw stones and yelled. The birds flew in all directions, trying to find a way out. One after another, pigeons started for the window. Seeing Little Bill, they would turn back and land on the unloading track running at the peak of the roof. Vera and I threw as hard as we could, but little arms are just not strong enough to propel a stone that high. Ken joined in to no avail.

Finally the birds were spooked into flight again. This time one headed for the window. Swish, it flew directly out without landing on the sill.

"Still lots more in here, keep yelling." Little Bill yelled.

Just then another pigeon flew toward the window, turned and circled, and then flew back to the window. This one landed on the sill. Bill lunged forward and grabbed it by the legs. He now had a pigeon and a problem! How could he hold onto a bird, with wings flapping, and still hang on to the beam so as to not find himself plunging toward the hay below. Finally, he managed to put the pigeon inside his shirt and re-button it. Now with both hands free he might be able to climb down without falling. Excitedly, Vera, Ken, and I waited on the roadway of the barn between the two haylofts. Soon Little Bill was down to the hay, and over to the ladder, finishing his trip to the floor. Opening his shirt we had our first good look at the pigeon—it was a beauty! It had a blue-gray back and a brilliant white underside. Its head and neck were an iridescent blue and green.

"Boy it sure is pretty," Vera blurted out, "but where we going to keep it?" Proud and happy we started for the house.

Meanwhile, the gasoline engine powering the Maytag ringer washer had drowned out the sound coming from the barn. Mother was unaware of the happenings. She kept hanging the clothes on the line that stretched across the back yard. We ran up to her and excitedly flocked around her.

"Ma! See what we got!" we all blurted out.

Wide-eyed with wonderment she asked, "Where did you get that?"

The story was soon told in complete detail. Throwing the handful of clothespins back into the basket, she barked, "You climbed up the side of the barn? You know you could have been killed if you'd fallen!"

"But Ma, there's lots of hay to fall on," Little Bill assured her.

"I don't care how much hay there is, don't climb up there again." Pointing at the pigeon, Mother barked, "No bird is worth it!"

"We're goin' to keep it! Can we?" Vera asked.

"Where? You can't keep it in the house!" Mother protested.

"We'll make a cage for it," Little Bill countered.

"You can put it in a cardboard box until your dad gets home. Maybe he'll make something for you to keep it in," Mother consented.

Her voice had calmed, and the kids knew the worst was over. Now past the shock, she helped put the pigeon in the box for safekeeping. Mother was becoming accustomed to the small wild animals we brought home: frogs, turtles, and polliwogs. What would these four energetic kids think of next? This capture had taken great effort, planning, and involved danger. To make matters worse, the fifth child was nearly big enough to join in the escapades. When Dad returned home from work, all four of us ran to the car. As he stepped from the car, he was immediately mobbed by excited kids.

"Dad, Dad, we've got a pigeon!" we all remarked. "Come see our pigeon!"

"Will you make us a cage?" asked Little Bill.

"Come on, hurry, Dad!" I said as I pulled on his arm.

We dragged him to the back porch. "Isn't he a beauty? Will you make something to keep him in?" Little Bill asked again.

"Just a moment, let me see your mother first. Then we'll work on something." Soon the excitement slowed. Mother had the evening meal in the warming oven of the kitchen range and was setting the table. "Right after supper we'll make a box for your pigeon." Dad promised.

"Do you have something to make it out of?" asked Mother.

"Ya, there's a piece of chicken-wire fencing and boards in the barn." Shortly after supper, the sound of sawing and pounding could be heard. The pigeon had a new home. "You can keep it for a while, but soon you'll have to let it go," Dad told us.

"But why?" we asked.

"You wouldn't like it if someone penned you up, would you? So someday you'll have to turn it loose."

Dad instructed.

"Okay," we agreed as we put the bird in the cage and placed it under the apple tree.

Evening was family time, so we all went outside for games. One of our favorites was a game played with tin cans, called "Duck on the Rock." It was a game all the family could play. The rules were very simple. It was basically a game of tag. Children invented many games like this. They could accommodate any number of players, whether young or old. Even little Francis could play! She would throw her can like everyone else, but it only went a short distance. A mock chase that really excited her would ensue. The game would go on until dark. Even Grampa and Gramma played.

"Time to stop," Dad would shout. "Pick up your cans and put them under the porch."

"Do we really have to quit?" we would complain.

"It's almost dark, so let's get going," Dad said.

We marched in the house and Mother would clean us up. After a little snack, off to bed we went. After, of course, we'd try our typical excuses of, "I'm not tired," and many others. The one that really caused a commotion was, "I've got to go to the toilet." The kerosene lantern would have to be lit, and either Dad or Mother would escort us down the path to the outside privy; the end of another summer day.

In the morning after breakfast, we all ran out the back door to see our pigeon. Turning at full speed I slipped and fell. I yelled with great agony as Mother came running out just as I was getting up. I had streams of blood pouring down my arm. She swept me up and carried me into the kitchen. She grabbed a dish towel and wrapped it tightly around my arm. Gramma appeared on the scene and along with Mother, pressed my arm to stop the bleeding. Soon it was under control. I had fallen on broken glass and sustained a deep cut an inch and a half long on my right arm. This curtailed my activities for the next few days!

One morning after recovering, Ken and I headed out to feed the pigeon. "Look at that! We're going to have a baby!" Ken shouted.

In our excitement we forgot about feeding the bird, and instead ran back to the house. "Ma, Ma, come quick, look what we've got," we yelled. Mother started toward the cage.

"Come on. Hurry Ma, you got to see it!" I shouted. Bouncing back to the cage we knelt down and peered in.

"Isn't it a beauty?" exclaimed Ken.

"Sure is," I answered back.

As Mother walked up we both pointed, "Look, we're going to have a baby!" Lying in one corner was a small white egg.

"How long before it will hatch?" I asked.

"Don't get your hearts set on it; it might not hatch at all. But we'll give the pigeon time; you'll just have to wait," Mother answered. That was the only egg laid and unfortunately it did not hatch. However, this didn't cool our excitement for the bird.

The day came when it was to be set free. All of us kids gathered around. Little Bill opened the cage, reached in, and lifted the pigeon out. All said our good-byes and he threw it into the air. It was free! It made a short circle, and landed back on the cage only to take off again circling further each time. Eventually it joined a group of pigeons flying overhead. For several days it would return, but never again did it become a captive.

This simple life was great for us kids. It kept us active, and through imagination we would amuse ourselves, though not always the way our parents appreciated. It did, however, hone skills that could be helpful later in life.

There were new activities for every season. In the winter, the family would gather after dark in the dining room. We'd sit in a semicircle around the wood-fired space heater. The sliding door between the living room and the dining room was closed to conserve heat. Mother or Gramma would sit in the old wooden rocking chair, while the other adults would gather around the dinning-room table and play cards or games. Dad and Grampa's favorite was checkers. The children played on the plain wood floor in front of the stove, or just sat leaning back on their hands mesmerized by the flames flickering through the small isinglass windows in the stove door. The warmth of the fire and crackling of the flames added serenity to the evening. With no electricity, radio, or television, and only a few commercial toys, the children would get out their homemade toys. A set of building blocks, a small wooden wheelbarrow, or guns whittled from wood. This taught social skills for adult life.

These were hard but simple times. If you wanted eggs, you gathered them from the chicken coop. If you wanted milk, you milked the cow. For water, you took the pail to the hand pump outside and pumped it. There were no demands on time for after-school activities. School was for learning the basics, and there was no hectic social schedule. Occasionally neighbors might drop in to visit. Evenings were mostly spent in family time that built strong ties. In our family, the children became downright clannish! We might quarrel among ourselves, but we would unite in defense of each other.

One day just before school, Little Bill beckoned Ken and me outside. "Would you to like to go fishin'?" he asked.

"Yea! When do we go?" we answered.

"Right now, you can fish for chickens. Go get the fishin' poles from the barn while I get some corn," Little Bill instructed.

Off we went, returning with the poles, and waited excitedly while Little Bill carefully removed the fish-hook. Then using a nail, he poked a hole through a kernel of corn and pushed the fish line through it and tied it securely. Handing the poles to us he said, "I'll scatter some corn on the ground and the chickens will begin to feed. Then you throw your line out. When a chicken picks up your bait, let him have it for a while so he gets a good hold of it. Then just pull up your pole and you'll have a chicken."

At this he disappeared around the corner of the house. We started fishing and soon caught a chicken. The fight only lasted a few seconds before the chicken let go.

"Ken, let the chicken swallow it, they'll fight harder," I instructed.

Each time a chicken was caught, and the corn pulled from its throat, it would cackle and cough. This drew some unwanted attention from Mother. Little Bill heard her coming out of the kitchen, and took off for the front yard. He left Ken and me with the evidence in our hands. "What do you think you're doing? Get those poles back to the barn!" Mother shouted. As usual, Little Bill was nowhere in sight, and missed his share of the scolding.

With no hesitation, we headed for the barn, poles over our shoulders, line flying out behind. Up the barn bank, in through the open door we went. There were a few chickens scratching for seeds and insects in the small amount of hay left on the floor. Ken swung his fishing pole and hit one of them; over it went. Regaining its footing, the chicken started for the door, but something was wrong. It couldn't walk on one leg! It did manage to drag itself outside.

"You broke its leg!" I busted out. "Now we're in trouble!"

Fortunately for us, the chicken turned north into the barnyard, not towards the house.

"We better not go back to the house right now. Ma'll kill us!" I warned.

We played in the barn for some time. Mother had returned to the kitchen, unaware of the happenings in the barn. When Dad came home that evening, Mother met him at the door. "I saw a chicken with a broken leg. Must have been hit by a car. Might as well eat it."

Ken and I looked at each other and said nothing. We quietly walked outside. "Don't think we should fish for chickens any more, and don't you break any more legs! Next time, Ma might catch us!" I said.

Memories

How long since we basked
by the stove burning wood?
Heavy-eyed, to bed we are carried,
as soon as they could.

Watched the Christmas tree twinkle
in a candle-lit room.
We're stopped running through
the house by a swish of the broom.

How long has it been?
Memories now still.

Country School

Cooler weather indicated the end of summer. Soon school would be starting and it was my turn to start school. The first day arrived! Bill, Vera, and I started the one-mile walk to school, lunch buckets and books in hand. Books were passed down from older to younger children within the family. If there were none to pass down, you could sometimes acquire used ones from a neighbor or at the bookstore. Only one store in town was appointed to sell schoolbooks.

Arriving, Bill and Vera greeted old friends. I met the other kindergarten pupils, Dan Matthews and Norval Fisher. I knew Dan as he lived about a half mile east of us and Dad did farm work for Hub, Dan's father. Dan and I would become good friends, and we shared many adventures, not all of which turned out well.

It was a great morning, and as always on the first day, the children built a fort in one corner of the schoolyard. The grass had not been mowed all summer and had grown to the height of about three feet. A few days before school started, one of the farmers had cut it with his team of horses and hay mower. At 10:30 a.m., the first recess started! The school soon emptied of students.

"Let's get our fort built!" the older boys yelled as they started for the wood storage behind the school. They'd scavenge any boards or large sticks that might be there.

"You girls and little guys start gathering all the grass you can," one of the older boys ordered. "Put that long board across the corner of the fence so we can lay the short ones on it," the assumed leader of the group barked out another order. Soon the children were all following the instruction the older boys were giving. The roof started to take shape as the grass was laid on the boards.

"How we goin' make the sides?" I asked.

"Just stuff grass into the holes of the wire fence, that'll hold it and make it look like a wall," was the instruction of the leader.

By now the other kids had gathered a large pile of grass in front of the fort.

"Take these boards and lean them up for the front," our leader ordered. Just then the bell rang, and recess was over.

"We'll finish at lunch time," was the word as we headed inside.

Lunch hour came and the kids headed out to finish their fort. The grass was placed on the roof boards and stuffed in the wire fence. There were boards leaned against the roof and down to the ground to form the front with a small opening for a door. Not everyone entered into the building process. Some of the older girls, twelve or thirteen years of age, were just too sophisticated for such a primitive venture and refused to help. Still, in a short time the entire frame was covered and it looked like a grass hut. Everyone tried to be the first in. It became the focal point for play as well as a great place to eat lunch.

The one-room Fisher School was like all other country schools—kindergarten through eighth grade all in one room with one teacher for all. The one-room concept was a great way to learn. Everyone was exposed to all of the classes, and it enhanced the learning experience. Discipline was strictly enforced. Kindergarten was a working class the same as any other class. The alphabet, numbers, and printing our name were taught.

Teachers were not only responsible to teach, but they also had to build the fire in the wood-burning stove for heat during the cold months. They kept the school clean, and helped with hot lunches that the community women brought in during the winter. The lunches consisted of one hot dish, usually mashed potatoes, soup, goulash, or something equally as nourishing. It tasted very good with the sandwiches from our lunch box.

The country school was like a big family; older kids helped the younger ones. Though there was an occasional disagreement, for the most part things went smoothly. The day started at 9:00 a.m. with the Pledge of Allegiance to the American flag, singing from the Golden Songbook, and sometimes the teacher would read from a classic like Huckleberry Finn. All this happened before study began. At about 10:30 a.m. there was a fifteen-minute recess and everyone had to go outside. Most entered into a team sport like softball or soccer. We went back to class until noon. Lunch lasted from 12:00 p.m. until 1:00 p.m. At 2:30 p.m. there was another fifteen-minute recess. Younger children, those in kindergarten and first grade, could start home at this time. The older children had to stay until 4:00 p.m. This was a typical school day.

Children going in the same direction to and from school walked together and had a good time playing along the way. One afternoon I had permission to stop at Dan Matthew's house on the way home from school. It was a bright and warm fall day. Dan and I walked along the dirt road, carrying our coats over our backs or swinging them in the air. We saw a car coming toward us and Dan burst out, "Throw your coat in front of the car." Without giving it any thought, I let the coat go. It landed directly in front of the car. The driver swerved to miss it and continued on, or so we thought.

When we got to Dan's house, Hub harnessed the team of horses and hitched them to a flat-bed wagon. "You boys want to go along? I've got to get some corn for feed," Hub asked.

Willingly we jumped on the wagon. I thought it strange that Hub grabbed a long-handled shovel before we headed down the lane. Why would there be need for a shovel? He drove down to the cornfield but didn't stop. Instead we headed for a pond at the edge of the field. As soon as the wagon stopped, Hub jumped off. He grabbed the shovel and started digging. It was evident now why he needed a shovel. Muskrats started coming out of the hole. As each one came out, he hit it with the shovel and threw it onto the wagon. Finishing, he threw the shovel onto the wagon. He covered everything with corn shocks. (People during those times did whatever they could to make ends meet. Muskrat pelts could be sold for daily living expenses.) Back at the barn, Hub quickly unloaded the corn and muskrats to be skinned later.

"Dan, you two let the sheep out of the barn for water," Hub ordered.

Dan and I headed to the sheep run in the basement of the barn and threw open the door. After picking up a stick, Dan jumped into the sheepfold and I followed. The sheep became very excited as Dan poked at them. They began running in a confused fashion, jumping over one another and bleating. In their confusion they could not find the open door; still Dan kept chasing! To our horror, one sheep collapsed on the floor as it tried to jump over another. It was dead as dead could be! In terror I jumped from the pen while Dan continued to poke at the sheep. Finally the sheep found their way out.

Deciding it was a good time to leave, before Hub found the dead sheep, I started running the few hundred yards home, my imagination running wild. Terrifying thoughts were going through my mind. What if Hub blames me! Dan might tell him I did it! Sheer panic gripped me as I raced on. I didn't dare tell anyone what had happened. It might get back to Dad or Mother! If it did, I would be as dead as that sheep!

All that evening I sat in suspense. I waited for that six-foot giant of a man to come and get me for killing his sheep. On into the night I agonized over the what-ifs. Of course none of them came to pass, but to a five-year-old anything seemed possible. The next day at school I asked Dan what happened when his dad found the dead sheep.

"Oh, nothin', he just butchered it, said we needed meat anyway."

I had the weight of the world lifted from my shoulders, what a relief! But it wasn't to last. As school started, Mrs. Fisher informed Dan and me that the driver hadn't just gone on the night before as we had thought but stopped at the school and told her about our coat-throwing exploit. This did not sit well with Mrs. Fisher. We lost our recesses for the day, and had to wait for the older children before we could go home that afternoon. Now, there was a strong pact between the Sprague kids. You don't tell on me and I won't tell on you. This way

Ma and Dad wouldn't worry about us. Dad and Mother never had to worry about this coat-throwing episode!

Thanksgiving and the Friday after was a two-day break from school. Activities in the classroom leading up to this holiday centered on the pilgrim's first feast. We were taught about their arrival in this country and why we should be thankful for what we had. Often there would be a party on the Wednesday afternoon before the break. The mothers would bring in cookies, cupcakes, or something equally delicious.

School resumed the following Monday, and the Christmas theme was introduced. This was a great time in the country school! Part of every day was spent practicing for the school play. The play was presented at the Christmas party, held in the evening of the last day of school before winter break. Anticipation and excitement ran high for the big event.

There was another cause for excitement at this time of year, the teacher's gift. The older girls usually organized the process of collecting money from children who could contribute. This particular year, when the money was counted, it was nearly four dollars. A lot of money for the times!

"How are we going to get to town to get the gift?" asked one of the girls.

"Let's ask the teacher if a couple of us can walk into town and purchase it," another girl suggested.

Mrs. Fisher agreed. "Two of the older boys can go;

you children choose."

Little Bill and Loren Lewis were picked and instructed to find an appropriate gift. Anything left over
might be spent on themselves as a reward for walking to
town. Bill and Loren made the three-mile walk to town.
After a long time looking, they finally both agreed on a
very inexpensive dish. Unfortunately this left most of
the money.

"They told us we could spend the rest on ourselves,"
Bill said.

"But do you think they meant this much?" asked
Loren.

"Sure," Bill assured Loren.

Both convinced, they bought and ate candy galore.
They ate so much they weren't feeling well by the time
they were ready to leave town. With money still in their
pocket, they decided to purchase another gift for themselves. Returning too late to go back to school, the boys
went home. Mother became suspicious, and started
questioning Little Bill. Discovering they had spent most
of the money on themselves, she was furious. Not only
had they broken the trust of the other students, but as far
as she was concerned they had stolen the money. Little
Bill was seriously disciplined, and told to apologize to
all when he got to school the next morning.

Bill and Loren had to face the wrath of all the students, and the discipline of the teacher. She assigned
additional chores: cleaning the chalkboards, dusting

the erasers, and mopping up the water from the snow that had been tracked into the school. The humiliation of standing accused before their classmates made both boys realize they had made a serious mistake!

The night of the long awaited Christmas program finally arrived. Families started coming to school about 6:30 p.m. Several of the community men had assembled the old board stage two weeks earlier. The children had been able to have a full dress rehearsal. The women had repaired the stage curtains and hung them on a tightly stretched wire across the front of the stage. It seemed the whole community was involved. The little children were ready, and nervously awaited their turn to recite their rhymes.

"Now don't be afraid, just stand behind this curtain and try real hard to be quiet," Mrs. Fisher would remind us.

The main play, as usual, was about the birth of Christ. Mary and Joseph had taken their places seated by a cradle filled with straw, with a doll lying in it. The three wise men came in and placed their gifts in front of the cradle, and Joseph slid his chair back to make room for them. As each came on stage, Joseph would say, "And what gift have you for the Christ child?" Each would recite what they had brought and lay it down.

After the wise men came the shepherds. In an effort to make room Joseph again moved his chair back a little further. The last poor five-year-old shepherd entered, carrying a large jar of colored water. He was easily distinguished from his historic counterpart. He wore a printed flour sack fashioned around his head and flowing down his back like a cape. He also wore patched, faded bib overalls and high-top shoes. The same question was asked of him.

"What have you brought for the Christ child?"

"I have brought some very precious perfume, and it smells like new-mown hay."

The audience began to snicker as the shepherd took a few steps forward to put his offering with the rest of the gifts. Now Joseph was about to learn why it is important to be able to estimate distance. Sliding his chair back once again, he was met by the harsh reality that he had run out of stage! One leg of the chair slipped off. Joseph, chair, turban, and cloak went sprawling to the floor amid hilarious laughter from the audience. As fast as Joseph hit the floor, he bounced to his feet, a little dazed but unhurt.

"Close the curtain! Close the curtain!" the teacher whispered loudly, trying to get the attention of the boys controlling the curtains. All of the children laughed uncontrollably as the boys frantically jerked the curtains together. In their haste, one boy stepped on the curtain and down it came. The whole house erupted with laughter. Meanwhile Joseph, not knowing what to do, took several deep bows, stalling for time to figure out how to get out of his predicament.

Mrs. Fisher, embarrassed almost to tears, composed herself. Smiling, she walked over to Joseph, put her arm around his shoulders, and announced the end of the program. There was singing of traditional Christmas carols. The teacher was presented with the gift from the children, and also one from the school board. In turn she had a gift for each child. The kids excitedly opened them.

Just at that time there was a loud, "Ho, ho, ho!" heard outside. The front door burst open and there was Santa Claus in his bright red suit, his large sack over his shoulder as he stepped through. The children flocked around him as he walked to the front of the room handing out small paper sacks containing popcorn, peanuts, and hard candy.

This brought to a close the typical Christmas program. As the people filed out, the oil lamps and candles were extinguished, the doors locked, and the last embers of the fire in the pot-bellied stove faded away. School would be in recess until the first Monday after New Years.

In the country school, the ethic of scripture had been reinforced by the code of conduct required of each student. The teacher had control without harsh measures. Consolidation into a large metro school system marked the beginning of the end of God in our schools. The message of Jesus was no longer presented in song and program at Easter and Christmas.

When we lost the country school, we lost the center of our rural community. This was a tragedy for the nation. I cherish the memories of rural life. Those fond memories shaped our lives. I was that last poor shepherd boy with the faded, patched bib overalls, and the perfume that smelled like new-mown hay. Though we as a community and individual families had next to nothing, we really had everything—we had each other!

Christmas marked the beginning of the return of prosperity. Grampa was feeling better, so he was doing light work. Best of all, his storytelling had resumed. Dad's work had improved to three or four days a week. The hourly pay was low, but all in all things were on the upturn. There was even talk about electric service coming to the area. Great, no more icebox, no need to store food in the cistern, and maybe even inside plumbing! However, this was not to be for a few more years.

The Sprague family Christmas that year would provide some commercial Christmas candy, a toy, and a coloring book for each of us. The best of all was a used snow sled given to us by a friend. Mother and Gramma, as usual, put on a great feast of roast goose with all the trimmings. One day during the Christmas break Vera and I took our new sled to a hill north of the barn. At the base of the hill was a large accumulation of snow over a ditch.

Pulling the sled to the top of the hill I suggested, "Vera let's slide down into the drift."

"Okay, I'll lie on the sled and steer it. You push us to get us going and then jump on my back," Vera replied.

I started pushing, and off we went! Faster and faster, the snowdrift was coming closer and closer. Then it happened; we hit the drift, snow flew in every direction, and Vera started crying. When the sled hit the snowdrift, it slammed into the frozen bank of the ditch. We were thrown into the snow. In the process, Vera cut her lip.

Picking ourselves up, we brushed off the snow and started for the house, Vera held her lip and I pulled the sled. The wound was not serious and by the time we arrived the bleeding had stopped, but her lip was badly swollen. Mother took Vera's coat off, checked to see the seriousness of the cut, and sat her next to the fire. It was decided sliding down the barn bank was much safer.

That night when the family gathered around the heating stove, Grampa stoked up his pipe and sat back in his chair. He stared off into space so we knew we were in for a good story. "You kids know how big your great grandpa Hugh was? He was six foot four and he weighed over two hundred and fifty pounds. Well, he was just as strong!"

Gathering close, two of us sat on the homemade foot stool and the others curled up on pillows at his feet. We were ready. Grampa puffed a few more times on his pipe and leaned forward and started his yarn. "The truth is he was so strong he could just take me and pick me right up with one hand and hold me right up in the air. Why I've seen him take a sugar beet and crush it with one hand."

Now our interest had been captured. We sat fidgeting in anticipation of the big story to come. "Well, one day when he was outside, he looked up to see a big deer head into the shed where the feed was kept. Now he wasn't about to let that there deer eat the cow feed. He just sneaked real quietly toward the shed, and around the end of the building he went. That big old deer never saw him coming. He was too busy eating all that cow feed! He must've been doin' it for some time, 'cause he was really fat. Well, Grandpa Hugh just kept sneaking closer and closer, but just as he got to the door the deer saw him coming. Now this deer was big. He had big sharp horns that stood high above his head."

Grampa held his hand with fingers outstretched above his head to emphasize his story of big horns. Dad sat quietly, smiling and thinking to himself. Grandpa Hugh could crush a sugar beet in one hand. He really did kill a deer in his woodshed with an axe, but who knows if it even had horns. The horns addition did add interest and sure kept the kids' attention.

Grampa stopped, reached over, and picked up his can of Union Leader tobacco. He opened it very slowly and filled his pipe. He packed the tobacco down with his finger, and then tamped it with a nail to stall for time. By now we could hardly stand it.

"Come on Grampa! What did he do? Did the deer get away? Hurry!" we all asked.

"Well, ya know that deer put his head down and started for the door. Your Grandpa Hugh put his head down and he also started for the door." Grampa stopped again, this time to light the pipe. He very deliberately stood up and got a match from his pocket and touched it to the hot stove. As the match burst into flame, he held it to his pipe, He drew heavily, until the tobacco glowed in the dimly lit room. Opening the stove door, he tossed the still-burning match into the fire. Sitting down he took a few more puffs. Leaning his head back and blowing the smoke into the air he watched it swirl upward. By now, we were fit to be tied.

Returning to his story he went on, "Grandpa Hugh was pretty fast in spite of his size. He just ran up to that door and slammed it shut. Now the deer was goin' so fast he couldn't stop. BANG! He hit that door."

A couple more puffs and a big smoke ring burst from his mouth. He watched it swirl to the ceiling.

"Come on Grampa, what happened?" we cried.

"Well, ya know, as big and strong as that deer was he couldn't budge that door with your Grandpa Hugh holding it."

"What did the deer do, did he get away?" Vera asked.

"He just kept butting that door harder and harder," Grampa went on. "Grandpa Hugh knew he was betwixt a rock and a hard spot; going to have to do something soon or that deer would break it down. As mad as that deer was, no telling what he would do if he got out. So, Grandpa Hugh just propped that door shut and went after the axe. When he got back he opened the door and went in."

Grampa stopped again to relight his pipe and puff a few more times. Standing up he headed for the kitchen.

"Got to have a drink," he informed us.

By now we were furious. "GRAMPA! Tell us what happened!" we all shouted.

Returning he continued, "Well there was a big battle! First the deer would have the upper hand and then your Grandpa Hugh; it just went on for hours. There was times your Grandpa Hugh thought he would just open the barn door and let that deer out, but he wasn't about to be beat by that thievin' deer. That deer made one more lunge for Grandpa. Grandpa saw his chance; he grabbed that there deer by his horns, and with one hand, threw him to the ground. Finally, he got that one blow with the axe and the battle was over. We had deer steaks for supper that night."

"Say, you guys, it's getting late and Mother thinks you should be in bed, so off you go," Dad instructed.

During the night the snow had drifted high around the barn bank. The next morning, it seemed like a good time to build a snow cave. Bill, Vera, and I, with shovel in hand and big plans in mind, took off for the barn. We would dig into the drift and make a snow fort.

Little Bill as usual took over. "Start digging right

here. Go straight in and don't break down the roof. It'll make a great cave."

Vera and I started digging with our hands as Little Bill scooped away with the shovel. "Don't do that—you'll cave in the snow roof! Vera you are just not doing it right!" Little Bill would say. After a lot of shoveling and scraping, the cave was complete.

Many days of entertainment for all of us were realized in that cave. The fascination of the cave increased when Mother entrusted us with a candle to use for heat and light. We ate snacks in it, and at times, just lay down and watched the snow sparkle as the light from the candle flickered away.

On our first day back after Christmas vacation, the children who had snow sleds brought them. We were so proud of ours! Recesses found all of us sliding down the road east of the building with those few sleds shared by all. When not sledding down the road, we would go to the small pond just across the road from the school—running and sliding on the ice, or playing hockey. No one had hockey sticks or pucks, but we used dead branches and a stone. Improvising was a way of life.

The next event in the school year was Valentine's Day—party time! We got one half-day off school for treats, games, and a card exchange. We made valentines for our mothers and bought or made valentines for each other. Mothers brought the treats, and everyone had fun.

The weather warmed and the snow melted; our lunch periods were spent sliding and skating on the only ice left—the small pond east of the school. The beginning of the warm weather alerted the farmers it was time to hang sap buckets; spring had begun. The freezing nights and warm days started the sap flowing in the maple trees. Wood had been cut earlier in the winter to be used for fuel to boil the sap into syrup.

Hub Matthews and Andrew Kennedy hooked up their teams of horses to a stone boat, placed a wooden barrel on it, and headed for the woods to collect sap. After that day's collection was complete they emptied it into the evaporator and started a roaring fire underneath. The work of boiling syrup had begun. Once boiling started it was kept going day and night until finished.

Community children flocked to the sugar shanty for a taste of freshly boiled syrup. We always took along eggs to boil in the sap for that sweet maple taste we loved so much. The men were congenial and even offered cups of half-boiled sap, a real treat. Andrew and Hub made sure we had homemade maple sugar candy, a highlight for all of us. Maple syrup was a source of revenue that helped buy seed for spring planting and, on a good year, earn extra money for the family.

The school ground was now too wet for softball, so the children played another game—it was called Anti-I-Over.

"Let's choose up teams for Anti-I-Over," the oldest

boys shouted. "We'll be captains."

With the team selected the game began.

"Remember you've got to catch the ball before you can come around after us. No cheating! You got to touch us before we have to be part of your team," the captains instructed.

With one team on each side of the school building, the predetermined team threw the ball over the roof to the opposite team. If the ball was caught, the chase was on. Around the schoolhouse came the players with the ball, tagging everyone they could before the other team got to the opposite side. The game ended when all of one team's members had been tagged, and made part of the other team, or when recess ended.

Soccer was another favorite! Whenever it was played, Louie Winslow was the one to have on your team. Louie had one artificial leg, and when things got tough, he would wade in with his wooden leg flying. It just plain hurt when it collided with your shin, so everyone would back off and let him have the ball.

The last day of school was a festive day for all, no schoolwork, just ball games and treats. The highlight was a wonderful potluck meal, with ice cream and lemonade. The whole community joined in, and another school year was over. Walking home, the carefree days of summer were already dominating our minds.

Summer Vacation

The first morning of vacation gave us children an opportunity to sleep in. After we awoke, we straggled one by one down the open stairway into the kitchen. Mother, very understandably, accommodated each of us with breakfast. It was to be a lazy day for all. After the usual romping around with the other children, I headed outdoors. Being inside on a bright sunny day was just not the place I wanted to be! On rainy days, I would stay inside playing the old foot-pump organ in the attic or playing checkers.

Down the kitchen steps I ran and out to the driveway. As my bare feet hit the gravel, I became painfully aware summer was here. Every year it started this same way, but soon, all of our feet would be like leather. Shoes weren't worn for play! In fact, they probably wouldn't be worn at all, not until school started again in the fall. Most of our shoes had holes in the soles, but still they had to be saved as they could be patched. We did this by placing cardboard inside over the hole. The cardboard didn't last long, but it sure was warmer and easier on the feet than the hole! There was also a possibility that Dad could get some leather and resole them before the start of school in the fall. It was intriguing to watch him place the shoes on the cast-steel anvil and nail the new soles on. We watched the dust fly as he sanded the edge of the sole to conform to the contour of the shoes, making them as good as new.

The fruit trees around the house had been in full bloom, but were now taking on a ragged look as the petals began to drop. Small fruit could be seen forming in the center of the blossoms. The large elm trees in the front yard had a green hue as the leaves burst from their buds. Ah, the sights and fragrance of spring! The sounds of frogs chirping in the ponds captivated me as I aimlessly walked around the yard. A robin landed in the apple tree near the chicken coop. "I'll see how close I can get to it before it flies," I said to myself.

Stalking slowly, and very deliberately, I headed toward it. My eyes were fixed on that bird. Placing one foot in front of the other I crept on, closer and closer, loosing my balance only to recover and keep going. It was as though I was stalking some big game in the wilds of Africa. Intensely, I kept my eyes glued on the robin. Great thoughts going through my mind, I imagined I was on a safari deep in the jungles of some far-off land. Now the quarry was almost at hand. Just a few more steps and that great bird would be mine, I thought. One step, then another, slowly, deliberately, and I was almost there.

"I can just about touch it. Should I grab it or just touch it and let it fly away?" As I reached out my hand, the great bird simply flew away. "Oh it's just an old robin after all, not some really great bird."

Then the call came. "Let's have a ball game!" Dad shouted.

"Yea!" could be heard from all over the house and yard.

Dad headed for the front yard, ball and bat in hand. In his youth, he had played ball in Flint, and he was quite a proficient player.

As the little troop gathered in the yard, he would hit the ball and all of us would run after it. A game of 500 began. In this game a fielder who caught the ball would receive points. Whichever fielder totaled five hundred points first would become the new hitter. The current hitter would go to the field. It was great fun playing with Dad and the other kids.

Sometimes a ball game called "work up" was played. It was some sight to see this rag-tag ball team: Dad, Little Bill, Vera, Kenneth—who was only four years old—and me. It was family time, so everyone played, not very well at times, but who cared? We were together! Now, whenever Dad or Mother was present, the ball game went very orderly. When just the children played, the rules, dictated by Little Bill, were very flexible. Needless to say, they would always favor him. Vera tried her best to have the same opportunity, but we boys would always taunt her.

"You're only a girl, you can't play ball as well as we can," or, "You can't hit the ball hard enough, so you just can't be the batter."

The same was true with the pretend game of Cowboys and Indians.

"Vera, you've got to be the Indian and get shot dead," we would taunt her.

Francis, who now thought she should play with the big kids, also had to be an Indian and the big loser, however, this was always done very democratically. Instigated by Little Bill, the three boys voted for the two girls to be Indians. Reluctantly Vera would give in. Francis, too young to understand, just didn't have a say. She was happy just to be part of the game.

Late spring and early summer was a great time living in the country. The high water in the ponds teemed with wildlife: frogs, snails, snakes, and muskrats. Rabbits hid in the tall grass around the edges. I liked to get by myself and walk about the ponds to watch the creatures, to skip stones across the water, and listen to the birds in the trees. Red-winged blackbirds, with their loud singing and undulating flight, inhabited the marsh across the road and around the small pond north of the barn. Meadowlarks, bob-o-links, blue birds, and robins were everywhere. The ever-present English sparrows, pigeons, and starlings frequented the barn.

It was fun catching polliwogs as they darted through the water. As always, a fresh catch of frogs and snails housed in a quart glass jar captured the attention of Mother as it showed up on the kitchen table. The biggest catch of all was a snake! This really excited her, especially when us boys put it in a box and kept it in the house. Mother was a good sport about letting us keep most of our trophies.

We spent hours playing in the sand that had washed down the incline of the driveway. Blocks of wood, stones, and tin cans became trucks and wagons. Occasionally we would have a real toy truck! Vera received a toy wicker doll buggy for Christmas but we boys thought it would make a great truck for hauling sand. However, filling it to the top and trying to push it in the loose dirt proved too much for the wire-spoked wheels. The sides gave way from the pressure, and the sand poured out as the wheels buckled under the load. Vera watched with disbelief as her prized toy crumbled beneath the stress.

"You broke my buggy!" she cried as she ran to the house to tell Mother.

Even with all of Dad's attempts, the buggy was never quite the same. Thankfully it would still carry a doll. It continued to serve Vera well, though the wobbly wheels and the unraveling wicker made it much less attractive.

Never again was it used as a truck!

One day while we were playing in the sand of the driveway, Dad returned home from work. We scurried out of the way as he turned the Chevy into the drive. I, out of impulse, ran out and tried to jump on the front bumper for a ride. Missing, I fell in front of the car. Dad was horrified as he felt the car ride over me. Jumping out, he picked me up and carried me into the house. My leg had been run over but a close examination revealed no broken bones, just badly bruised. Another good lesson learned: never run in front of a car!

Some weeks, Dad would get extra work in town. He'd earn an extra three or four dollars, money that could certainly be used. We were told that if everything went well the family could go to see Grandma Mary in Lansing. It would be the first time out of Barry County for any of us children, except Little Bill. It would be the only time he was old enough to remember.

Soon the great day arrived. We were in the car, with a packed lunch and water, and whatever else Dad and Mother thought was necessary for the trip. The excited children, all trying to talk at the same time, were making Dad a little nervous.

"Quiet down you guys," Dad cautioned.

The excitement was overwhelming, and containing us was next to impossible. The old Chevy rambled down the dusty gravel road, and as the novelty wore off, the bickering began. It was stopped by a second sharp and very stern warning. We all knew better than to resume, so it quieted for a while. One hour then two, and finally the city appeared in the distance—Lansing at last! We all peered out the windows; our eyes had never seen anything like this. In wonderment we all just stared at the buildings and all those people!

Kenneth soon broke the silence, "Look at all the chocolate-drop people!" (It was the first time any of us children had seen someone of another race.)

"They're black people," instructed Mother.

"How did they get so black?"

"They're born that way," Mother explained.

"Why?" was the next question from Ken.

"The world is made up of all kinds of different-looking people," Mother came back.

"Why are they made different?" Vera asked.

"Just the way God made things," Mother replied. This didn't really satisfy our young minds, but we accepted it and were soon on to other subjects of equal interest.

Arriving at Grandma Mary's, we jumped out and stretched. It sure felt good to get on solid ground again. It had been the longest ride of our lives, but we had survived the ordeal with the help of the lunch and naps.

This was to be a real learning experience for Ken and me. Shortly after arriving, Aunt Pearl and Uncle Ernie Wilson and their children came to visit.

"Ronnie, would you take Tom and Ken with you and

go to the store and get some things?" Grandma Mary asked, handing him a list and some money.

Boy, going to the store was going to be quite an experience, we thought. It turned out to be even more of an experience than we had anticipated! We headed out the door and down the sidewalk, talking and laughing as we skipped along. It didn't take long until we arrived at the little corner store.

"Not much bigger then our chicken coop," I said, "but there's lots of things I've never seen before!"

The grocery list was purchased and we headed home. We had no more than started, when four boys about our ages approached. They seemed friendly enough, so Ken and I started talking to them, for some reason though our cousin Ronnie seemed very nervous. Out of nowhere, something hit me squarely in the face. These friendly boys were not so friendly after all; now we knew why Ronnie was nervous. By the time the stars stopped shining in my head and I could see again, the strangers had vanished.

"I though they might do that!" Ronnie burst out. "They're the toughest kids around! They just like doing mean things and then running off."

Lesson one about city life: always keep more than an arm's length between you and those you don't know. Whatever else you do, don't turn your head!

Sure is some strange way to live—I'm not sure I like this town, I thought. City people are not the same as good ol' farmers! You didn't have to worry about anyone you played with back home hitting you without some good reason. I thought maybe we had made a mistake coming to Lansing; for sure it was a mistake to go to the store.

We walked into the house with the groceries tied with string in brown craft paper and set them on the table. Mother looked at me and asked, "What happened to your face?"

"Oh some boy hit me when I wasn't even looking and all I was doing was talking to him," I complained.

Just then Dad walked in. "Tom, one thing to remember when you're in the city: don't trust every kid you see. Some kids are always looking for trouble. Hoping to find someone that doesn't know what's going on, so they can pick on them. It's not like home."

Our cousins Ronnie and Harvey grabbed their bats and ball. "Let's play ball," Ronnie called, as they bounced out the door to the yard. That was just fine with us country boys; no strange people were going to get to us there.

That night there weren't enough beds for us all, so we used blankets on the floor for beds. We were so tired after the events that sleep would not be long in coming. After the usual bickering among the siblings, all was quiet and sleep set in.

The next morning, Ronnie got me alone. "Come on, I got something that's lots of fun, lets go."

We went out the door to the bank of the river where

no one could see us. Ronnie reached into his pocket and pulled out a pack of cigarettes. "Here Tom, try one," he said, as he took one for himself.

Slipping one from the pack, I put it into my mouth. Striking a match and lighting the cigarettes, we puffed away as the smoke flowed freely.

"Ron, I'm not feeling so good; I'm sick," I said.

"Put out the cigarette and lie back on the ground. You'll feel better in a couple minutes," Ronnie explained.

"I don't dare go home like this! I'll just have to suffer it out until I can walk without throwing up," I said.

Minutes seemed like hours, yet the sick feeling would not leave. Finally after about an hour, I figured I could make it back. I'll stay in the back yard where no one will know how I feel, I thought. If I just sit out here very quietly, maybe my stomach will be all right. That was the only time I ever tried smoking—once was enough!

This was the first of the many trips our family made to Lansing. Adventures to Potters Park for a ball game with older cousins, uncles, and friends made for very pleasant outings. The park, in the 1930s, was a city park with ball diamonds and picnic areas. It also had a wild-animal park, like a zoo, with a few monkeys, a buffalo, a lion, and not much else; but it was fun. Ball games and picnics with the extended family—what could be better?

The two-day weekend soon ended, and we found ourselves in the old car rattling down the dusty road toward home. We kids felt mixed emotions; we'd had fun but getting back home on familiar ground would sure be nice. There we could romp through the fields and watch frogs in the ponds. We could just lie back and watch the clouds drift by without the sounds of the city to break the silence. Dreams of great conquest and far-away adventures could go on without interruption. Fatigue and the sway of the car took its toll. Soon there was silence as all of us fell asleep.

The following week, Gramma and Grampa moved to Podunk Lake west of Hastings. They planed to stay there the rest of the summer in a large canvas-wall tent. Gramma's Indian background had taught her how to live off the land. They planned to eat primarily fish, frog legs, roots of aquatic plants, young tender dandelion greens, and wild horseradish. Whenever Dad and Mother went to see them, they supplemented this diet with a few canned goods: a little fresh meat, milk, butter, eggs, tea, and coffee.

The dirt road to the lake was narrow and hilly. We enjoyed the sudden loss of gravity, as Dad would speed up the car whenever he saw a hill ahead that dropped off sharply. While at the lake, we fished and swam. It was a great time! On occasions one of the older children, Little Bill, Vera, or I, could stay with them. It was the highlight of our summer. A week of swimming, fishing, and our grandparents all to ourselves! Along with the fun came a great education about survival by living off the land.

They showed us that a campsite needed to be set up well. We needed a fire area that included a rack to hold a few essential cooking utensils, a large tin can to make a smoke smudge, a pail for water, and a washbasin. Grampa also taught us how to store the bait and the fish. He made two boxes of wood and wire hardware cloth and placed them in the shallow water of the lake. One held the fish they caught until they were ready to be cleaned and eaten. The other held minnows and small frogs used for bait. One of the first orders of every day was to catch the bait, and we were allowed to help. They taught us which bait was used for which fish and where to find it. We also learned where and when we were most likely to catch our limits.

Bass fishing required a frog about two inches long, hooked through the jaw with a number 2/0 fishhook. Using a cane pole with black fishing line, Grampa taught us to cast the frog into the weed patches at the shoreline. This is where a largemouth bass would most likely be. Early morning and evening were the best times for fishing. Oh how I liked the fight of a big bass! Swimming in and out of the weeds, they would pull so hard I could hardly keep the pole upright.

We learned that through the day, fishing for bluegills with worms was very effective. Crickets, grasshoppers, and white grubs also worked great. Worms were easy to find. We dug for them in the moist dirt along the shore. Catching crickets, on the other hand, was a challenge! They hid beneath anything on the ground with room to crawl under, and we had to grab them quickly as we removed the cover before they scurried off into the grass. White grubs were found in the pasture under dried cow dung. Gramma and Grampa had a wealth of knowledge that fascinated us and endeared us to them as they patiently taught us their skills.

When evening came the mosquitoes presented quite a problem, but Grampa and Gramma had the answer. To control them, they built a small fire in a tin can, then packed green grass over it, and took it into the tent. The smudge would kill the little tormentors, or drive them out. I tried to go in the tent to get the smudge, but all that smoke just made my eyes water, and tears ran down my cheeks. Smoke got in my nose causing me to sneeze. It was no wonder the mosquitoes got out of the tent!

Summers in that old canvas tent taught us a way of life few will ever experience. The love that was shown to us by Gramma and Grampa during those pleasant warm days, along with the knowledge we absorbed, created some of our fondest memories.

Memories

How long since we splashed in
puddles and rolled in the grass?
Tin cans were our toys,
and stick swords did clash.

We hid in the granary, or jumped in the hay.
Wandered in woodlots and fields all day.
Built dams in the streams to hold water at bay.
Caught frogs in the ponds, made mud into cakes.
Chased snakes in the fields
and fished in the lakes.
Swam in the swamps and sledded on the hill.
Picked wild berries and ate our fill.

How long has it been? Memories now still.

The Sprague family around the year 1938.
Back row: Marie Miles (cousin), Vera, Little Bill
Front row: Francis, Ken, Tom

The author's sisters, Francis and Vera Sprague - 1937.

Bessie and Libby Sprague

Here are my grandparents, Bessie and Libbie Sprague
around the year 1945

Fisher School - State Road, Hastings, MI
Middle Row: #1 brother, Bill Sprague Jr. (Little Bill)
#4 sister, Vera Sprague
(school year 1935-36)

Little Bill   Vera

Author
Tom Sprague

Ken   Francis

Altoft School - 1939-40 school year
This was the only year all five Sprague children
were in the same school.

Thelma and Bill Sprague Sr. at their
50th wedding anniversary

VOLUNTEER ENLISTMENT.

STATE OF   TOWN OF

Maine   Shapleigh

I, Hugh S. Sprague born in Bethlehem in the State of New Hampshire aged 18 years, and by occupation a Farmer Do HEREBY ACKNOWLEDGE to have volunteered this Seventeenth day of March 186 5, to serve as a Soldier in the Army of the United States of America, for the period of THREE YEARS, unless sooner discharged by proper authority: Do also agree to accept such bounty, pay, rations and clothing, as are or may be established by law for volunteers. And I, Hugh S. Sprague do solemnly swear that I will bear true faith and allegiance to the United States of America, and that I will serve them honestly and faithfully against all their enemies or opposers whomsoever, and that I will observe and obey the orders of the President of the United States, and the orders of the officers appointed over me, according to the Rules and Articles of War.

Sworn and subscribed to, at Portland   Hugh S. Sprague
this 24 day of March 1865.
Before Charles H. Doughty

I CERTIFY, ON HONOR, that I have carefully examined the above named Volunteer, agreeably to the General Regulations of the Army, and that in my opinion he is free from all bodily defects and mental infirmity, which would, in any way, disqualify him from performing the duties of a soldier.

Chas W. Thomas
EXAMINING SURGEON.

I CERTIFY, ON HONOR, That I have minutely inspected the Volunteer, Hugh L. Sprague previously to his enlistment, and that he was entirely sober when enlisted; that, to the best of my judgment and belief, he is of lawful age; and that, in accepting him as duly qualified to perform the duties of an able-bodied soldier, I have strictly observed the Regulations which govern the recruiting service. This soldier has Grey Eyes, Brown Hair, Light Complexion, is 5 Feet 10½ Inches high.

15 Regiment of Maine Volunteers,
Charles H. Doughty RECRUITING OFFICER.

Mustered into the service of the United States, in Company the 24 day of March 1865 at Portland _____ 15 Regiment of Maine Charles H. Doughty Colonel Vol.org.gov

Great Grandfather Hugh Sprague's enlistment papers
into the Union Army during the Civil War

Great grandfather Hugh Sprague's Civil War drum

The author's older sister, Vera Sprague, when they were still children. The author wrote the following poem titled "*Vera*" in honor of their relationship.

Vera

You were there when I first saw light.
You stared wide-eyed wonderment and delight.
When I first learned to stand,
you helped me with outstretched hands.
We romped and played on wood floors so cold.
Not too rough, you can get hurt we were told.
To the outdoors we ventured to play in the sand.
We ran over the lawn to explore our land.
Then there was school and my first day.
You again were ahead and paved the way.
Teen years, high school and war, we did not part.
Then entered two that stole our hearts.
Our marriages just two weeks apart.
Throughout the years, you were always in the lead.
Now it's my time out front in your time of need.
To show you the one with the outstretched hand.
For only He can lead us to that promised land.
If you should precede me, it's not by chance.
Just look over your shoulder, take a glance.
I'll be just behind, it won't be long.
Age and time, I'm no longer strong.
Together again, where we'll never grow old,
Nor will we play on floors that are cold,
but we'll run and skip on streets of gold.

The Dare and Skunks

The old hip-roof barn was the scene of many a day's play for us kids; it had always been considered a safe place. The small granary in the end of the hayloft, when not in use, made a great pretend playhouse. Vera, Little Bill, Ken, and I were busy playing in the loft with what hay was left from the winter, when Bill came up with what he considered a great idea.

"Say Tom, why don't you get up on the granary and jump down on this pile of hay?" Little Bill asked.

"I'm not going to jump on that little bunch," I protested.

"Awe, you're just scared to," Bill teased.

The others joined in, "Tom's a fraidy cat, Tom's a fraidy cat, he's afraid to jump."

The granary was about eight feet tall. Jumping from the top of it had been fun when there was a lot of loose hay to sink into as you landed! Now there was hardly any left, but I wasn't to be shamed. "If you'll gather all the hay and put it over here in one pile I'll jump."

Even with every bit scraped and stacked together, the pile was still small. I tried to reconsider, but the others kept taunting. I was not to be branded a "fraidy cat," so I climbed slowly up the loft ladder to the top of the granary. I hesitantly stepped off onto the granary roof. I walked over to the edge and peered down. The pile of hay looked even smaller than it had from the floor.

"Come on jump! Don't be a baby, fraidy cat, fraidy cat," came the chant. "Tom's afraid to jump, he's afraid to jump, fraidy cat, fraidy cat."

I stared at that small pile of hay that just seemed to shrink smaller and smaller. I wasn't going to back out now. I would not be known as a baby! So with one last deep breath and closed eyes, I jumped into the air. Panic gripped me as I fell to the hayloft floor hitting with a hard thud. Then pain shot up my leg! I rolled over and grabbed my ankle, while the tears flowed and a great sob escaped my lips. I had missed the tiny pile of hay and landed on the uneven wooden plank floor. Dead silence engulfed the others as they stared at me with wide-eyed shock.

Vera finally broke the silence. "Better get Mother!" she screamed as loud as she could, starting for the house. "Mother come quick, Tom's hurt! Tom's hurt!"

The kitchen door burst open and Mother rushed out yelling, "What's wrong?"

Vera tried to explain that I had jumped and hurt myself, but in her excitement she couldn't make it clear to Mother. Vera turned and headed back to the barn.

Mother arrived on the scene and quickly summed up what had happened. She checked the leg. Relieved there were no broken bones, she scooped me up in her arms and carried me to the house. After reassuring and comforting me, Mother started questioning the others.

"We don't know, he just jumped! Next thing he started crying!" Little Bill explained.

"But he missed the pile of hay," Ken burst out.

"You mean you had him jump off the granary? He's lucky he didn't break his neck!" she snapped.

Knowing the culprit, Mother turned to Little Bill. "Billy, you know better than to get one of them to jump from there! Don't let me catch any of you jumping like that again!"

Mother wrapped my ankle with a cloth soaked in cold water, and soon the pain started to ease. The voice of experience had spoken loud and clear once again. The little troop had survived intact after another mishap! I was greatly curtailed for a while, but soon it was over and forgotten—the adventures resumed!

One evening while Dad and Mother were sitting on the front porch, Hub Matthews came walking up the driveway leading a large brown dog. Dad recognized it as Red, one of two dogs he and Hub hunted raccoon with.

"Evenin' folks. Bill, I have to get rid of this old dog,

two's just too many to feed. Thought you'd like to have it. That way we can still have the two to hunt with," Hub said.

"Sure, I guess we could take him," Dad replied.

That's how Old Red became a member of the family. He was a good playmate for us kids, even though he led us astray on several occasions. One time I remember he discovered skunks in an abandoned barn across the road. Since we boys had become a little bored on this particular day, we were ready for something to spice up our lives.

"Let's go over to the barn across the road and watch the baby skunks," suggested Little Bill.

"That'll be fun, let's go," I answered.

Off we went with Old Red bouncing through the tall grass ahead of us. The skunks were in the basement of the barn, so we went up the barn drive to the second floor hayloft. Several of the floorboards had rotted and fallen through to the basement below. We lay on the weak floor and quietly peered down at the young skunks as they ran about unaware of our presence.

"Let's get a stick and poke 'em!" Little Bill suggested.

"But Bill, won't they squirt us?" I asked.

"Nope, they won't know where we are," Little Bill whispered as he quietly slipped outside and got a long stick.

Returning, he pushed the stick down through the

hole in the flooring and started poking at the black and white critters. They turned and raised their tails, but there was nothing to squirt. It was great fun until Old Red charged into the basement straight for the skunks! They were primed and ready. Up went their tails and this time there was something to squirt—Old Red! The aroma was overwhelming; it permeated everything, including us!

"Oh, let's get out of here!" Ken said as he pinched his nose and headed for the door.

Outside we became sick to our stomachs.

"What we goin' to do now?" I asked. "Ma's not going to like this."

Old Red headed for the pond and splashed in. The skunks had hit him square in the face and eyes. He rolled in the water and rubbed his eyes with his paws. Coming out he headed directly to the house.

"Oh, I hope he doesn't try to get in," Little Bill remarked.

Sure enough he went straight to the back door, but luckily the screen was closed. Mother, smelling the dog, chased him off. Meanwhile, we were also heading for the kitchen door. Mother smelled skunk again and turned to the door to chase the dog away again. Instead of a dog she found three smelly boys.

"What have you boys been into this time?" Mother barked.

Sheepishly the story was related.

"Billy, when are you ever going to stop and think about the things you do? I don't know how we'll ever get rid of this awful smell. Take your clothes off and I'll get the washtub. You guys are going to get scrubbed before you come into this house!"

After a good bath of tomato juice, a thorough washing with lye soap, and a rinsing with cold water, the smell was a little better; at least enough so we were allowed in.

Romance and Christmas

It was to be Kenneth's first year of school. His enthusiasm was somewhat dampened by the many exaggerated horror stories from us older kids. Kenneth always reacted in the same way. "I'm just not going!" he would cry out.

The day arrived with all its excitement and, with Mother's insistence, Kenneth did join us and our friends on the one-mile walk. All of us neighborhood kids had missed each other during the summer. A buzz of chatter filled the morning air as we caught up on all that had happened during vacation.

Also starting kindergarten was a pretty blonde girl named Marilyn. Ken was about to experience a new emotion; it was love at first sight. Kenneth and Marilyn spent all their free time together. At the first sound of the recess bell they would start out, hand in hand, to the woodshed attached to the rear of the school. Alone there, they would talk, kick the wood chips, and throw small pieces of coal around. There was no attempt to mix with any of the other children! This went on for several days. We teased them unmercifully and continually invited them to play with us, but nothing could persuade them to give up this relationship. Teasing from all of us at home didn't affect Ken, and nothing deterred him from spending all the time he could with Marilyn. Puppy love had blossomed! Gradually as time passed and the weather turned cold, their love cooled as well. They began playing with the rest of us. Puppy love had faded!

Ken was not always easy for a teacher to handle. He did not enjoy school enough to want to stay cooped up in the building all day. One morning, experiencing an unusually strong feeling of confinement, he jumped up and shouted, "Bill, I'm going home!"

To the disbelief of all the children, and especially us Sprague kids, he headed for the front door as fast as his little legs could carry him. Down the cement steps and out to the dirt road in front of the school he raced, heading for home. Mrs. Fisher was racing right behind! He gave her a good run, but he just wasn't fast enough. Grabbing him by the shirt collar, she turned him around and headed him back to school. At the moment the teacher's hand grasped his shirt, gravity lost its power. Ken's feet were having trouble touching the ground! With the hold on his shirt firm, she dragged him back kicking and yelling. Going up the steps and into the building, his toes never touched the cement. Flying through the door, gravity regained its power as his feet finally landed on something firm. Mrs. Fisher proceeded to apply the rule of law in the traditional manner of the day—a few hard swats on his lower anatomy. As he was marched to his seat he again lost the effects of gravity. Only the tips of his toes were able to reach the floor. Gravity finally returned with all its force when he was thrust into his seat.

"Now stay there," commanded Mrs. Fisher. Needless to say, the rest of us were model students the rest of the day. We knew those same rules of law applied to us!

Ken started each new school year, grades K through 6, the same way. It seemed he had to test each teacher to find just how far was too far. Each responded in like manner. Once the line had been established, Ken would go right to it and maybe even stretch it some until reminded; then he would back off.

With the holidays approaching, practice for the school Christmas program was in full progress. At home, Christmas was the topic that captured our every conversation. Montgomery Ward and Sears and Roebuck Christmas catalogs stemmed dreams for things we knew we could not possibly afford. Pleasant thoughts of the brightly trimmed tree and the good food that was part of the holiday celebration were ever present in our minds.

The excitement of receiving was modified by the requirement that each child had to sort out one or more toys, in good condition, to be given away to someone less fortunate. Even though we sometimes only had one, it had to go if we were to receive another. This was Dad and Mother's way of teaching us not to be selfish. Our parents tried to instill in our minds that no matter how bad off a person was, if they would take the time and look around, they could always find someone less fortunate.

Christmas Eve arrived and the house was filled with the smells of pies baking and a goose roasting in the oven. During that long day, the wood box at the end of the wood-burning kitchen range always seemed to be empty. The call would come, "Tom, I need more wood."

Out to the yard where Dad had split and stacked the winter's supply, I'd go. I'd brush aside the snow, gather an armful of wood, carry it back, and stack it neatly inside the wood box. This ritual was repeated several times during the course of the day.

Darkness came, and with it, bedtime for the children. After Mother and Dad thought we were asleep, they started trimming the tree and arranging the gifts underneath. Meanwhile upstairs, when we were supposed to be in bed and asleep, we were actually taking turns peeking though the slightly opened door. We tried to observe everything in the dining room below. Light from the flickering oil lamp reflected from the glass tree bulbs and tinsel. Heat from the wood-burning stove stirred the air just enough to create movement of the aluminum icicles and spun-glass angel hair. The whole tree twinkled like little fire sparks in the night. The glistening trimmings appeared to be moving about the tree. Soon the whispers and giggles became louder with our excitement.

"You kids get in bed!" the command from Dad that startled us from our concentration on this magical scene. The shuffle of little feet could be heard and everything quieted, only to be repeated two or three more times. Finally Dad's voice took on an unmistakable tone, and then there was silence!

Early the next morning, about three o'clock, the sound of our little feet was again heard on the floor. There was no stopping us this time! Down we came with wide-eyed wonderment. Christmas morning had finally arrived!

Dad got up, stoked the stove with a few pieces of wood, and opened the draft. Mother lit the lamps and candles. We could see it all: the tree with its glistening beauty, the colorful paper of the gifts, and the wool stocking hanging on the wall bulging with peanuts and homemade candy. The joyous day had begun!

We opened our gifts and played for a while before breakfast. Fellowship with the extended family came with the big meal that followed.

Because we had risen so very early, fatigue set in not long after sunset. One by one we dropped off to sleep on the floor, or in a chair, and Dad carried us up the stairs to bed. We slept, clutching our new toy, replaying the wonderful day in our dreams. Soon even adult eyes were heavy; it had been a long day for them as well. The excitement had taken Dad and Mother's minds off the drudgery of surviving the depression that engulfed the country; they were now relaxed and for one day. All was well.

The Move

In the early spring of 1939, Dad and Mother heard of a twenty-acre farm for sale, three miles from where we were living. It wasn't much! The barn was old and in need of repair, as was the house, but it was something they could afford—nine hundred dollars. They had to borrow the one hundred dollars for the down payment. Mr. Gross, the owner of the company where Dad worked, offered to give him an advance on his pay. He could repay in small amounts each week without interest. All was settled, the contract signed, and the farm was ours!

This started an intense work schedule for our parents and grandparents. After getting us kids off to school each day, Mother and Gramma began the cleaning, painting, and wallpapering of the entire house. Evenings Dad and Grampa did the repairs that were needed. This continued until late May when school was out; then we all had to help!

One day Mother, Gamma, and Vera were in the house working when a man came down from upstairs. They were shaken badly until they realized he was the previous owner and was harmless. His mind had failed him in his old age. In his mind he had returned to his home and was now aimlessly wandering around. It wasn't long before someone looking for him arrived. They explained to him the house no longer belonged to him and he would have to leave with them.

The adventure of a new house excited us children, but the thought of moving and leaving our friends weighed heavily on our spirits. Vera was particularly troubled. All she could think about was never making new friends. (She did make new friends, of course.) One happy thought for the Vera and Francis: they would have a bedroom all to themselves.

It was great fun to explore the buildings and see all the old things lying around, discarded wrenches, parts of horse harnesses, and many other items that had been used on the farm. There was even a horse still in the barn that had not yet been moved. We spent hours out there talking to this gentle old animal. One of his hind hoofs was elongated about six inches, making it difficult for him to walk. This condition was commonly referred to as a box-stall hoof.

On the loft over the roadway of the barn, we found a horse-drawn sleigh, some old farm wagons, and broken-down horse-drawn implements. We soon realized the barn had to be put in order and the fences mended before Bessie the cow could be brought and housed here.

The henhouse was littered with chicken cages, laying nests, and broken roosts; all this had to be cleaned and repaired. The barn and hen-house were infested with rats, but the cats soon took care of them. After we finished cleaning both the barn and the coop, Dad disinfected them. One nice thing, there was a windmill to pump the water, if the wind was blowing. This saved us boys a lot of work during the cleanup, and certainly would on washdays, not to mention watering the cow, pigs, and chickens.

All was prepared and we were ready for the final move. Our uncles helped load our belongings into a borrowed wagon pulled behind the old Chevy. A rickety old trailer with high sides was used to haul Bessie the cow. Chickens were put in burlap grain sacks and moved in the trailer as well. Everything was now at our new home. The next several weeks were spent unpacking and arranging.

We kids now had time to explore all the land. This included the large pond in the pasture, the small drain ditch, and the four-foot square culvert that went under the highway. Each of these became favorite places to spend vast amounts of time.

Spring's beautiful clean greens added a newness to life as nature began its replenishing process in the grasslands and wood lots throughout the countryside. The grasses of the pastures were growing fast. All around the edge of the pond was a new growth of cattails and bulrushes. Wild purple flags (wetland version of wild iris) dotted the western shore of the pond and added color. Frogs were in abundance in the pond and the pasture. Their constant chirping sounds filled the night with song.

Hunting frogs was a new adventure that came with our new home. We cut two holes in the side of a five-pound cloth sugar sack, then slipped our belt through the holes to make it easy to carry. We tied a pair of shears on the other side of our belts, found a stick just the right length and shape, and off we went. The plan was to hit the frog with the stick to kill it, then use the shears to cut off the hind legs. We would put the legs in the sugar sack. Over the years we lost many pairs of Mother's good scissors in the fields. We spent hours frogging with great success; it was nothing to catch a hundred or more. After we finally returned home we skinned and washed the legs and Mother rolled them in flour and deep-fried them. They made a great meal. We watched in amazement as the frog legs would kick and move in the fry pan as the heat caused the muscles to contract.

With all the new adventures and new places to explore, the summer came to an end too soon. School was about to start. This was to be Francis's first year and Mother was feeling bad that the last of her babies was leaving for school. That first day of school we discovered that the Altoft country school was larger than the Fisher school both in the size of the building and in the number of students. Altoft had over forty students that year with just one teacher for all of our nine grades. Mrs. Brown was very capable of handling us; her secret weapon—control!

Kenneth was not too sure that Mrs. Brown's resolve to maintain order could be obtained, and as usual had to find out. The third day of school, he decided not to come in from recess. She started looking and found him hiding in the outside privy. Marching my reluctant brother inside, she proceeded to apply her hand of authority. Not to be out done, Ken started spanking her! Mrs. Brown's strikes started getting harder and harder. Ken's best judgment told him it was time to quit. He accepted his just reward.

With school in session, I wanted my ball and ball bat for the ball games we played at school. I started looking for them. Search as I might, they were not to be found. After several days it dawned on me where they were; I had hidden them from Little Bill in the back corner of Mother and Dad's bedroom closet. They were in the house we had just moved from, and they were never retrieved!

Frost had turned the tree leaves to their fall beauty, marking the beginning of hunting and trapping seasons. Dad had promised to teach us how to trap. We boys became anxious for a new experience, trapping in our very own pond, which was full of muskrats. We each had received a pair of green-laced rubber boots for this very purpose. Gathering our traps, the four of us set off for the pond. Dad had pointed out muskrat houses, runways, and feeding stations. Taking a trap and setting it, he started explaining how to make the set.

"Now if you set the trap in too deep of water he'll just swim over it without being caught. See right here is a good spot, not too shallow, 'cause if it was you'd get him by the front leg, and maybe the leg would break and pull off before he drowns. It has to be just right so you get him by the hind leg, then he can't get away, and will drown right away. Remember the law, no set less than six feet from a muskrat's house or hole," Dad explained.

Once on our own, we did not always closely follow the law. We discovered it was much more effective if the trap was placed inside the house or at the very mouth of a hole. We ran our trap line in the morning on the way to school, which didn't prove to be a good idea. Little boys and water almost never mix well. Inevitably at least one of us would fall in, get wet and muddy, and have to return home for dry clothing. Mrs. Brown was very understanding and just endured without saying a word. On the days no one got wet we carried our muskrat trophies to school and left them outside to be carried home at lunch break, but not before they were admired by curious onlookers at morning recess.

To the dismay of Mother, and even more so of Vera, we had to skin the rats and stretch the pelts over a wooden board to dry. For Vera, who at the ripe old age of eleven was thinking of herself as somewhat sophisticated, it was appalling that we wanted to hang the pelts in our bedroom. The aroma of drying muskrat pelts is not always pleasant!

Vera, very correctly, said, "They stink!"

To Little Bill, Ken, and me they smelled like gold, money hanging from the ceiling, the sweet smell of success. Trapping became a large part of our lives, and as we grew older, the trap line expanded to cover several ponds and two lakes. I started at one end of the trap line and Ken at the other in order to be able to cover it in one night. The proceeds from trapping would buy our school clothes, fishing tackle, or whatever else we wanted for outdoor sports.

The move to our own small farm had brought many changes in our lives. Change was also taking place in our country. Preparation for defense of our country had started our economy on the road to recovery. Although the building of war machinery was met with some resistance, most realized that as Hitler marched his German army across Europe it would soon bring us into the conflict.

With the improved economy and our nation still at peace, Dad's work in town also picked up. Most weeks were now forty hours. There seemed to be a real promise of a better future. The coming Christmas would be one that brought relaxation without the money worry. Previously Christmas gifts were of a strictly practical nature, with maybe a toy or two to be shared by all the children. This year each of us boys received a BB gun, each girl a doll, and for the combined family an electric train! Wow, what treasures!

The Sleigh Ride

The first snow brought the excitement of sliding downhill. It was Saturday, and the three Sprague brothers were playing with our friend, Bill Barber. We were looking for a fun way to let off a little excess steam that had accumulated during school. For four country boys with a sense of adventure and a lively imagination, this was hardly a problem. As usual, Little Bill had a suggestion that would provide excitement to remember for a lifetime. "You know that horse-drawn sleigh on the loft in the barn?"

"Ya," we all answered.

"Why don't we get it down and take it over to Newton's hill and use it for a sled?" Little Bill suggested.

We all agreed and were off to get it. Now, lowering it from the overhead loft was no small task, but with the aid of a rope it was soon on the barn floor. We jumped onto the sleigh, and were off to the sliding hill. As the rust wore off the runners it became surprisingly easy to move.

"Looks like it's gonna slide good!" I remarked.

"Yea! Think it'll go all the way across the field?" asked Ken.

"Dunno. Maybe if we get a good 'nuff start," our friend Bill Barber said.

Newton's pasture had the biggest hill around, and in the spirit of the day, it was open to all the neighborhood children. Back then, folks were expected to have a little common sense and look out for themselves. If they didn't, well, consequences were how you learned common sense. No one worried about kids having a little innocent fun, or about the two massive trees at the bottom of the hill. Kids just pointed their sleds to miss them! If they got off in the wrong direction, a good sledder could swerve around the trees, and a bad one could always roll off.

Arriving at Newton's hill, Little Bill took charge. "Okay, let's push the sleigh over there. That's the best run. Just aim so it goes 'tween those trees," Little Bill commanded.

Newton's hill was high and steep, and the two large trees at the bottom of the hill, well, they were only about fifty feet apart.

A good sledder with a good run down the hill could exceed twenty miles an hour on an ordinary sled. Anticipation was high to see how the fast-gliding sleigh would do. The sleigh had only one seat, so the two larger boys got in first, then Ken sat on Bill Barber's lap. As for getting the sleigh started, Little Bill had that all figured out too. Ken was too small, and of course there wouldn't be enough time to make the double-decker seating arrangement on the fly.

"Tom, you get us goin'. Then jump in on my side here, and I'll pull you up. You can ride here on my lap," Little Bill instructed.

The flight plan settled, I grunted the sleigh into motion, and dashed around the side of the slow-moving craft. I scrambled up with Little Bill's help. The launch was executed with perfection. The sleigh exceeded our best hopes—it was fast! As the speed picked up, we were soon moving too fast to jump out. Unfortunately, about the time our velocity reached that point of no return, all four of us could see that the flight engineer had made a slight miscalculation. We were not headed between the trees after all!

"Lean to the right!" Little Bill shouted.

All of us shifted our weight as far as we could, and held our breath. The sleigh started to turn just a little; would it work? The sleigh scraped past one giant tree at highway speed and splintered a wooden bar that stuck out just past the edge of the frame.

Coasting to a stop beyond the trees, one shaky voice managed to squeak out, "Boy, that was close!"

"Yea," said Ken, "let's try it again!"

We turned the sleigh around and started the long

struggle to the top. After a mighty effort, and a few rest stops, we regained the summit. "Let's not try goin' there again!" Bill Barber suggested.

"Okay, we'll just head down there where it's clear sailin'," Little Bill agreed.

We aimed in a safe direction, and it wasn't long before we were all aboard and being hurdled toward our favorite goal—common sense. About half way down we struck a rock, tipping the sleigh up on just one runner. Now, if leaning was good for a little mid-course correction, well, coming up on one runner could make that old sleigh just turn on a dime! We swerved directly toward the woven-wire fence. We were going way too fast to jump out, so all we could do was just hold on and prepare for the crash landing.

We careened into the fence about mid-way between posts. The fence stretched to its limit, and stopped us momentarily. Then it threw us back like a giant slingshot. On the return trip, the sleigh shot upward flinging us against the sides of the sleigh. When it returned to earth, the sides instantly gave way on impact, spilling out boys like a ripped gunny sack gushing corn.

Dazed and bewildered, we picked ourselves up. We each tested our limbs for broken bones. Providentially, the casualty list was short: several bruises and four spinning heads. Not a bad price for common sense! Looking around at the debris, a new fear settled in.

"What's Pa going to say? I wonder what's he goin'

to do to us! I wonder what he'll do to me!" Little Bill worried. There was only one thing to do! The sleigh—or rather what was left of it—had to go back to the loft. More than a few grunts and groans later, made all the harder by our bruises, we had the wreckage hoisted back to its rightful place on the loft.

The next morning at breakfast, as always, there was a large meal of eggs, toast, and either sliced potatoes, fried potatoes, or hash browns. Dad made toast in the oven as the toaster just wasn't large enough to keep up with the demand, and he would often be distracted. Sitting down to the meal, tension was high; would our pact—you don't tell on me, I don't tell on you—hold? We all sat very quietly hoping Dad hadn't found out our secret.

Just then Vera took a big bite from a golden-brown slice of toast, "Oh Dad! You did it again!" That golden toast was burnt black on the bottom side, and as usual Dad had buttered the good side.

He just laughed and said, "Scrape the black off and eat it."

That broke the silence; all was well. Not one of us said a word about yesterday's adventure, and it was years before anyone raised a question about the sleigh's condition. So it was that we narrowly missed a painful end to our exploits.

That evening the family gathered around the radio to listen to our favorite programs: The Shadow, Fibber

McGee and Molly, and others. However, the only thing being broadcast this Sunday was news about the Japanese attack on Pearl Harbor. Sunday, December 7, 1941 was a day to be remembered; we were at war. This was the beginning of the end for the innocence of the five clannish Sprague kids, and the isolationism that had been our way of life.

Every family in America was affected by rationing of gasoline, meat, sugar, and by the shortages of just about everything, as well as by the drafting of our young men for military service. Several of our family were included in that number. The demands put on those of us left at home were accepted without complaint and we all did our part. We purchased war bonds through payroll plans, and war stamps, which sold for ten cents each. We pasted these stamps into books that when full were traded in for a bond. This made it possible for everyone to help with the war effort. People who never before raised a garden now grew a "victory garden." The country-school children gathered dried milkweed seedpods, and the seed chutes were used as filler for life jackets. Some knitted squares to be sewn into blankets for the military. Factories that had been idled just a few years before in the Depression were pushed to capacity, and Dad found himself working from 7:00 a.m. until 9:00 p.m. To help in the war effort many women went to work in the factories. All did what they could to bring this tragedy to an end.

Summer Exploits

Spring of 1942, there was still a chill in the air as Dad said, "Let's go." He had decided to buy a horse for fieldwork to raise our own livestock feed for our two cows, two or three calves, pigs, and chickens. We started on our way to see Andrew Kennedy, to buy his old black mare named Doll. It was about three miles to his farm. As soon as we arrived Dad and Andrew harnessed Old Doll and hitched her to a wagon. With a few instructions from Dad, I climbed up onto the bench seat and picked up the reins for the drive home. Ken was sitting behind me on the floor as we turned out of the drive and rattled down the gravel road.

I was proud as a peacock as I sat there on the seat, holding the reins and thinking I was in control. Of course, Old Doll didn't need any steering. She just trudged straight down the road. She was a gentle and dependable giant. As we bumped along, the seat on the wooden-wheeled wagon and its plank bed got harder and harder. So we shifted around but when that didn't provide any comfort, we stood—which isn't too easy in a horse-drawn wagon on a bumpy road. Ken and I were thrown this way and then tossed the other. Eventually, we decided it was best to just sit back down and take the hard knocks as they came. At last we made the final turnoff from Davis Road to the state highway. There was just one mile to go. Uncomfortable as it was, it was a thrill to drive the horse all by ourselves. The ride ended as we turned into the driveway at our house and stopped at the gate going to the barn. Dad came out and took Doll the rest of the way to the barn to remove her harness. The horse was kept inside the barn that night giving her a chance to get used to the strange surroundings. Meanwhile, I was occupied with strutting around and bragging about the feat of driving this great steed all by myself!

We planted corn in the field next to the school that spring. When it grew tall enough, I got to ride Doll and guide her down the rows as Dad handled the one-row cultivator. It was a lot of fun. That old mare became part of the family. Days when we were not working her I would go to the pasture and talk to her and stroke her muzzle. I liked that old horse. Later, years after we quit working her, she became a lady of leisure.

With the warmth of spring our BB guns were put to good use. English sparrows were considered a nuisance, and we boys tried to remove as many as possible. The birds roosted in the large maple trees across the road from the house, so after dark, with BB guns and flashlights, we headed out to shoot them. Francis was recruited to hold the light while Ken and I did the shooting.

"Fran, hold the light still and keep it on the birds," was the constant instruction we shouted to her.

"You just don't hold it right. There I missed another because of it!" I complained. Fran did her best, but at five years of age, it was a struggle, especially when her heart was not in the shooting of the birds in the first place.

With the acquiring of the BB guns we could change our way of frogging. One of us carried a BB gun, the other a stick or a frog spear. Frogs could be shot a distance far greater than could be reached with a stick or spear, greatly increasing our efficiency. When Fran wanted to go along, she was required to carry the sugar sack and scissors. Soon she too became a proficient frogger.

Our new house was located close to three lakes, and Dad started taking us kids fishing. First came the purchasing of cane poles, black fishing line, hooks, sinkers, and bobbers. It required selecting just the right pole, not too long, not too short, and with just the right action. Then we were off to the lake.

Fishing from shore produced an abundance of blue-gills, along with a fair share of tangled lines and, "Bait my hook, Dad." He enjoyed it anyway, and we loved it! Soon Ken and I were allowed to walk to the lake and fish on our own. It was some sight, the two of us in bib overalls and straw hats, fishing poles over our shoulders, and a can of worms in our hand, walking down the road to our favorite fishing hole. It was great sport, but getting the fish home in a condition fit to be eaten was a challenge.

Carrying them on a stringer in the hot summer sun dried them rapidly, so we dragged them through every water puddle along the way. Problem was we quite often dragged them on the dry, dusty road the rest of the time. Those poor fish would be like leather by the time we arrived home! Still they were cleaned, and after soaking them overnight Mother fried them.

Ken and I were always looking for a way to make some money. Men who worked with Dad ask him if he thought we would be interested in digging earthworms for their fishing trips. We jumped at the opportunity. Soon others were asking. As the demand grew, we decided to put out a "Worms for Sale" sign and launched ourselves into a business that demanded nearly full-time digging. Dirt worms sold for twenty-five cents a hundred and red worms for fifteen cents. Weekends and holidays we asked the whole family to help us dig. Little did we know that in years to come we both would make our living in the sporting goods business.

With the proceeds from the summer worm sales we

purchased our school clothes, and still had money left to purchase a pup tent. It was the beginning of great adventures. First we slept in it under the oak tree north of the house, then camping near Lower Lake for the opening days of bluegill season. But for now summer was over. Frogging, fishing, swimming, climbing in the barn, and playing in the hayloft had to be left behind; school was about to start.

The Vacation

The following spring plans were made for our first vacation. Grampa, Gramma, Dad, Mother, and four kids planned to head for Arnold Lake located about 120 miles northeast of home. Elaborate plans were made to ensure an adequate supply of canned food, cooking utensils, and other necessities. Our grandparents' large wall tent was big enough for everyone to sleep in. The rowboat, hauled on a trailer, would carry the camping gear, leaving all of the space in the car for people.

Finally the great day arrived, the boat was placed in the trailer, and the equipment packed into the boat. What we couldn't get in the boat, we squeezed into the trunk of the car. Then we all got in. The car was completely full with four children and four adults. Little Bill had talked Mother and Dad into allowing him to stay home, a decision they later regretted. After what seemed like forever we finally arrived at the lake. Thinking back, it probably seemed even longer to the adults with all of us squirming, excited kids constantly fussing and asking, "How much further?"

Locating a place to make camp, with a good swimming beach and lots of ferns, we started unloading. There was no way for the boat to be launched at this campsite because of the high bank. It had to be taken around to the public landing site. After it was unloaded, Gramma, Ken, and I rowed about three-quarters of a mile back to our camp. Meanwhile, the rest of the party was busy setting up and organizing. When we arrived with the boat, Dad put all of us children to gathering ferns to cover the tent floor. Blankets were then placed over the deep piles of ferns, making a good, soft bed. A fire pit was cleared, and the wooden boxes containing the camping supplies and cooking utensils were placed conveniently around it with a good supply of firewood. Mother and Gramma finished making the beds, and all was ready.

We couldn't wait to get in the water! With a lot of splashing and laughing, our fun began. It promised to be a week of immense enjoyment, great fishing, good weather, and lots of swimming. Evening came too soon that first day, but most were ready for bed. Dad built a smudge fire in a tin can and put it in the tent to control the mosquitoes. It worked great, and soon, even the adults drifted off to sleep.

The next morning we were eager to get started, and immediately after breakfast we kids headed for the lake to swim. Dad and Grampa, nearly as excited, set off to fish. By noon we were ravenously hungry and were ready for a break from the water. Mother told Dad it would be a good time to eat some of the fish and if he and Grampa would clean them we could have some for lunch. That was all it took and soon the fish were cleaned and ready for the pan. The fire was blazing, and the fry pan sizzling. Within a matter of a few minutes the delicious smell of the freshly caught fish frying over the open fire increased our already intense hunger pangs. Quickly we were all seated on the ground carefully picking out the small bones from the fish, and we filled ourselves to capacity.

Mother required us to wait an hour after eating before we could go back in the water. When that hour finally dragged by, Vera, the only one of us who could actually swim, set about teaching Ken and me. "First you have to learn to hold your breath. Now lie down in the water. Just lie there holding your breath," Vera instructed.

With this mastered, we started to kick our feet and soon we were moving slowly about. It wasn't long and we were both swimming dog-paddle style reasonably well. Next morning while we were swimming, Dad came down to the lakeshore with his cane fishing pole. Casting his line out just past the drop off, he caught a fish. Immediately we all realized it wasn't just any old bluegill.

"Acts like a bass," Grampa remarked.

The struggle to land it began with Dad getting it close to shore only to have it make a run for the deep.

After several minutes it was beached and Dad grabbed it before it could flop back into the water. "Boy what a beauty, I never caught a bluegill this big before," he remarked.

He took it to the tent, got a yardstick and measured it. Fourteen and one quarter inches! Putting it on a stringer and heading back to the lake he resumed fishing. It was just a few minutes and he had another fish on. "This one is acting the same as the last one," Dad hollered.

Again the fight was on. Into the shallow water then back to the deep. Dad just had to let the fish go where it wanted. Gradually it tired and Dad landed it. It was another big bluegill! Not quite as large as the first one, but much larger than the average. This one measured over twelve inches. Dad placed it on the stringer with the first one; it was an impressive sight.

That evening, after admiring the large gills one last time, they were added to the fish fry. We discovered after returning home that the fourteen-and-one-quarter-inch bluegill would have been a state record! Instead, it was eaten for supper.

The week was warm with lots of sunshine. Ken and I did some fishing with Dad and Grampa. Mother and Gramma fished too, but mostly just relaxed during this overdue rest. Vera and Francis practically lived in the water and when they tired of it, they just lay on the beach. We all spent a lot of time in the water; Mother told us we were in danger of becoming waterlogged! Evenings found us around the campfire listening to Grampa and Dad talk about the good old days, and of the fishing they had done when he and our uncles and aunt were growing up in Bay County.

The week was great, one that would be remembered, but like all good things it came to an end. Too soon, we were breaking camp, cleaning the site, and loading up for the long trip home. The ride found us kids too tired to stay awake and finally late in the evening, the folks woke us as the car pulled into our driveway. We climbed out, stretched, and began carrying things to the house.

Little Bill was not home, but it was evident he had spent time there—he hadn't taken care of a thing he had used. Mother was really put out. Little did she know the worst was yet to come! Little Bill returned later in the evening; Dad thought he had been drinking. Further questioning revealed he had been with the Newton twins—not good news. These boys were much older and always in trouble with both their mother and the law. As the questioning became more intense he admitted he had ordered fireworks through the mail—illegal in itself—then while riding with the Newton boys, had thrown firecrackers out the car window onto Main Street in Hastings. Of course, the police caught them and ticketed the Newton twins; they let Little Bill off with a warning because of his age. Needless to say he received strict discipline at home that didn't prove to deter him much.

Growing Pains

The next morning after returning home from vacation, Mother checked the garden. Weeds had taken over. She called Ken and me together. "I would like you two boys to weed the garden. The hoes are in the garage and you better get it finished before it gets too hot." Unhappily we started to the garage for the hoes.

"I'm not going to spend all day in this garden!" Ken said.

I tried to encourage him, "Ken, if we work hard it won't take long, and we can get out of here."

"I'm not goin' to work hard either; it's too hot," Ken remarked as he started hoeing.

I scolded, "Ken, you're not getting all the weeds."

"I know, but it'll take too long if I get them all," Ken complained.

"But Ma'll kill us if we don't," I said.

"That's good enough. I'm done!" Ken barked.

"You can't leave yet, we've hardly started," I

warned.

"Well, we better get done soon," Ken came back.

The hoeing continued slowly along with Ken's grumbling, and as the morning wore on the sun warmed up. The perspiration ran down both our brows. Ken was trying hard to think of some way to get out of this disagreeable work. Thinking of nothing to make it faster or easier, he stopped, looked at me, and threw down his hoe.

"That's it, I'm done! It's good enough!" Ken exclaimed. With that Ken started across the garden to the road, heading for the neighbor's.

"You better get back here; I'm not going to weed all the rest of this alone!" I screamed at him.

"Don't have to, it's good enough," Ken said as he reached the road, and was off on a run.

Looking over the garden, and seeing weeds in some places higher than the plants, I angrily went back to hoeing. "That Ken has left me to clean this garden alone again, and Ma will never say a thing to him either! But boy if it's not weeded, I'll be in trouble. She'll say, you're the oldest, so you should have stopped him. Fat chance of that," I grumbled to myself.

As my anger mounted, my hoe hit the ground harder, and the dust flew! Finally, the last row was finished. Picking up both hoes, I took them back and put them in the garage and headed for the windmill. The wind had picked up and the pump was flowing a large cool stream of water. I put my head under the spout. The water ran down over my face and chest letting it cool my temper as well as my body. I cupped my hands and caught water for a drink.

"Boy I'm glad that's over, wait 'til I get that Ken," I muttered to myself.

With all the pressure brought to bear by me and by Mother, Ken never did finish a hoeing job. He always thought, "It's good enough!"

As the hot, dry days of summer continued, Ken and I took note of the fact that the pond in the pasture was drying up. "Tom, if the pond dries up the muskrats will leave and we won't have any place to trap," Ken said.

"Ya, and no trapping, no money," I agreed. "I got an idea; let's dam the drain ditch coming out of the pond."

"Okay, how do we do that?" Ken asked.

"Just shovel sod from the pasture into the ditch until it's full. I'll get the shovels from the garage," I explained.

"Ya think Dad will care?" Ken asked.

"Na, if the water can't run out the ditch, it'll stay in the pond so the cows will have plenty to drink and we won't have to pump water for them either," I said.

"Ya, and the muskrats won't leave. Besides it'll make good skating this winter," Ken reminded me. "Just think of the money those rats will make us!" Ken continued. That decided, we walked through the pasture and down to the ditch.

"How about here to make the dam?" I asked.

"The ditch is a little wide here; let's go a little closer to the road," Ken suggested. We both agreed on a good place and dug out chunks of sod and carefully laid them in the ditch. "This is just not working! The water's washing these chunks away as fast as we throw them in."

"Lets just dig and stack a big pile of sod right here beside the ditch and then put it in all at once," I suggested. We finally got the pile ready and Ken started throwing them in. "Ken, you're not throwing it in the same place every time and it's wasting it."

"Well you're not even hitting the bottom of the ditch!" Ken complained.

"This isn't working, I'll get down in the water and you hand me the sod as fast as you can," I instructed, as I slid down the muddy bank to the bottom of the ditch. "Now hand it down."

After pushing several pieces tightly together, it began to hold back the water flow. As I wallowed in the ditch bottom it got muddier and muddier, just like thick soup. Still we kept going.

"Put some on this side where the water is going through," Ken instructed.

"Hey, you threw that piece so I couldn't catch it," I hollered as the water splashed us both.

The building went on for what seemed to us forever, and we were both getting tired.

"Think it's high enough?" Ken asked.

"Sure, it's almost to the top of the bank," I assured him. It was getting harder to walk in the mud so I dragged myself out. "We better put more sod behind the dam so it'll be stronger, don't you think?" As we both threw more sod in, the water splashed wildly. "Ken, you're throwing so hard, we're getting soaked," I said.

"No I'm not!" Ken came back.

"Ya, look at us. Ma will have our hides!" I said as I held out my shirt. Let's go down to the pond and wash ourselves; we can stay there until we dry out and Ma will never know.

We went to the pond, waded in, and began washing off the mud. The more we washed and moved about, the muddier the water became. Most of the big chunks of mud came off our bib overalls, but we weren't a pretty sight, to say nothing of our tennis shoes!

"Think Ma'll will see our pants are dirty?" Ken asked.

"Not if we stay away until we're dry and it won't take long in this sun," I assured him.

When our clothes got somewhat dry we headed back to the house. Mother was busy with the evening meal when we entered through the old weather-beaten back door and went up the steps to the kitchen. Hearing the "squish-squish" of our muddy, water-soaked shoes she turned from the kitchen counter just as we entered. Silence! We stood side by side, bib overalls stiff with dried mud and the "sweet" aroma of stagnant swamp filling the room.

Mother turned her back on us so as not to laugh at the pathetic sight. "I've been washing today, and I still have one more load of your Dad's work clothes. Just take off those dirty overalls and put them in the washer with his things."

We seized the opportunity and dashed through the kitchen and up the stairs to our bedroom.

"Boy are my socks black," I said as I took off my shoes.

"Mine too, and look at my underwear, think Ma meant to change all our clothes?" Ken asked.

"Boy, we better! How we goin' to hide this underwear from her?" I asked.

"Let's just roll it up in our overalls then she won't see it," Ken said.

We returned to the kitchen with our neatly rolled bibs overalls with our underwear inside. "Just take those overalls to the basement boys and put them by the washer," Mother said. She laughed to herself and thought, it wouldn't do any good to scold them; they'd just cause me more grief. Besides, it wouldn't prevent another escapade. Some things just have to be endured when you have a pair of active boys.

The pond gradually filled. With Francis tagging along, Ken and I decided to head across the pasture to the dam to see how it was working. "Look at that, it sure is holding," Ken said.

"Ya, the muskrats must love it!" I said.

The water in the pond now covered the weeds. The high water would hold the rats and when it froze in the coming winter it would make good skating as well. But there was a problem. The dam had also backed water onto Walt Johncock's fields upstream. Walt was not as impressed as we were by our first attempt at civil engineering. He allowed the dam to stay over the winter, but in the spring he opened the stream to dry his field so he could plow. This started an annual cycle: in the summer we built the dam, and the following spring Walt knocked it down.

With the dam holding, the water stopped flowing through the culvert under the highway. It was great fun to walk through it and be in there when cars rumbled overhead. The remaining small mud puddles harbored frogs, snails, salamanders, and all kinds of creeping life that we found fascinating.

Now Fran wasn't quite sure it would be fun in there. "But Fran it is fun, just listen to those cars going overhead!" we tried to reassure her.

"Well okay but not alone, and don't you leave!" Fran said as she went inside. "It's muddy in here, I'm coming out!"

"You can't come out until you catch something, even a frog!" Ken remarked.

"But I can't catch anything, they're too fast!" Fran came back.

"You better or you're not coming out!" Ken threatened her.

She didn't think she could catch anything, but she also knew all too well that we usually stood behind our threats! So with a little encouragement and the occasional threat, she complied and grabbed for the closest thing to her. Splashing in the puddle she finally caught a frog and triumphantly came out, soaked and covered with mud. We knew we were in trouble as soon as we saw her condition.

"You're so wet and muddy; you better get to the house and clean up. We'll keep the frog for you," I told her.

"We better not go up for a while; maybe Mother will forget about this if we stay away long enough," Ken said.

We let the frog go and strolled around the pasture until we began to get very hungry.

"Think it's been long enough?" Ken asked.

"Sure, it's gotta be safe now," I assured him. As it turned out, it was safe.

After finishing chores one particularly hot afternoon, Ken went to the well for a drink of cold water. The windmill was running hard from the steady breeze. Not wanting to pump water by hand, he decided to let the wind do the work. In order to make this happen, he had to slip a pin through the hole in the rod from the windmill as it lined up with the hole in the pump rod; then the wind would pump the water. Not finding the pin, he stuck his finger through the holes and immediately pulled his hand back and clutched the bloody finger. Running around to the side of the house where Dad was on a scaffold residing the house, he held up his finger.

"Dad, look what I did!" Ken called out.

Dad jumped down from the scaffold, swept Ken up, and rushed him into the house, shouting, "Thelma, come quick! Kenneth cut off the end of his finger."

They wrapped his hand in a towel, and off to the doctor they went; in due time they returned with Ken's finger heavily bandaged. He had not pushed his finger far enough through the holes to cut the bone, only the flesh on the very end. It was very painful, and slowed him up for a few days.

One day after his finger had healed, Ken and I headed to see Bill Barber, a friend of ours who lived just across the road from the Altoft School. The State Highway Department had been cutting trees along the road in preparation for hard surfacing. In front of the Barber home lay several poles, about six to eight inches in diameter.

"Let's build a raft," Bill suggested.

The three of us, along with Bill's friend Don Roush, got to work. We carried the pole-sized tree trunks to the large pond across the road. Now, freshly cut trees are heavy, and it was a struggle to get them to the pond.

Sometimes all four of us had to carry a single pole. After a fashion the task was completed. The process of tying the poles together with rope finished, we were ready to lunch the raft.

Then we had a new problem. It hadn't occurred to us how we would launch our craft. Try as we might, we couldn't slide it into the water—it was just too heavy! There was nothing to do but take it apart and reassemble it in the water. Our shoes came off and we started the chore all over again. Finally, success!

"We're ready to set sail," Bill stated triumphantly.

Pushing the raft to deeper water, we all tried to get on. As each climbed aboard, the raft sank a little deeper. By the time we were all on, it was well under the water line.

"That's okay," said Don, "It's not on the bottom."

We pushed off with a stick into deeper water so as not to drag bottom, however we rode still lower in the water and, because the raft wasn't very wide, it was tipping dangerously with our every movement.

"Quick! Stand in the—"Bill tried to warn us, but it was too late! The raft tipped up on its side and dumped all four of us unceremoniously into the pond. Thrashing about, trying to find some footing, we made a mental note that green poles don't float very well, and narrow rafts are unstable too! Ah, good ol' common sense. We gained a little more that day.

Well, it was a warm summer day, so we figured we

might as well swim. This worked up the silt on the bottom of the shallow pond, and the muddy water had an unpleasant swampy odor. When we tried to dry ourselves and get presentable enough to head home, we just couldn't get rid of that smell.

Arriving at the house we were met with, "What have you been doing? Just get those clothes off and get cleaned up!" Mother shook her head and walked away. Past experience had taught her not to overreact. This wasn't the first time that her boys had come home a mess!

The Fishing Adventure

Ken and I had been planning a fishing trip with our new tent. We had invited our two cousins, Ron and Harvey Wilson, to join us. Being city kids they really didn't have a clue as to what they had agreed to.

Before we could leave Ken and I had to prepare our business. Remembering how busy we were in previous years on opening day of fishing season, we spent our time digging worms to stockpile for June 25th, opening day. We had to have plenty on hand, since we would be away during the first few days of the season. We had plans to stay at Lower Lake for a week. It was to be an experience we would not soon forget.

When Dad arrived home from work, we were packed and ready to go. Loading our gear in the car we headed to the lake. Assured that all was set up properly, and with the usual last words of caution, Dad returned home. The sun was drifting low in the western sky and a chill was setting in.

"Let's build a fire," Ken said.

After all, what's camping without a campfire? Off we went to the small wood lot nearby. We brought back all the dead branches we could carry, scraped dry leaves and grass into a pile, and carefully placed dry twigs atop them. Everything was ready for the match.

"Someone get the matches!" commanded Ron.

Scrambling through the paper sacks of provisions, they were soon found and the tinder was lit. A blaze started flickering up through the twigs.

"Better get some large pieces of wood on there," I said.

So we all busied ourselves breaking up the rest of the sticks and piling them on the blaze. It grew larger and larger, but to our amazement, the dry, dead wood didn't last long. A heavy dew was forming on the grass. We needed more wood, so back we trekked to the wood lot. Darkness had settled in by now and our one flashlight with weak batteries was of little help. Still we persisted, and returned to camp with another armload.

Now all our clothes were soaking wet from the dew and the slight breeze was sure making us uncomfortable. The chill had penetrated our bodies and the only thing to do, of course, was to build up the fire. This accomplished, we gathered close to it to get warm. Soon our clothes were steaming from the heat. It felt good. First we stood facing the fire to warm our front side. Then, we turned to warm and dry our backs. We rotated like grilling chickens on a spit for about a half hour.

Our clothes were not quite dry, but our bodies were finally getting warm. Looking around for wood, we were shocked. Surprise, surprise, it was gone! So, we went to gather more!

The dew was even heavier this time out and we were getting even wetter than the first time. Building up the fire and doing the rotating game of roasting our front side and then our back, we finally warmed up. Again the fire grew dim and chill overcame us.

"Only half hour before daylight," Ken stated. It couldn't have been much more than midnight.

"Think we should get more wood?" Harvey asked.

"We're going to get mighty cold if we don't!" I commented.

So we went through the endless cycle again, gathering wood, drying clothes, soaking up the heat in our cold bodies, and going back for more wood. The few times our clothes actually dried, and we got warm and still had a few glowing embers remaining, we would lie down and talk about the fishing to come in the morning. There was no sleep for any of us weary wood hunters that night!

Finally the sky lightened in the east. Tired and hungry we started preparing breakfast.

"Where's the fry pan?" Ken asked.

"In the box in the tent." Ron said.

As Ken started searching, Ron got out the eggs and the lard. Harvey and I put the last of the wood on the fire. Gathering a few stones we placed them in a small ring close to the fire to hold the fry pan up off the blaze. Soon the eggs were sizzling.

"Where's the salt?" Ken asked. A search was started.

"No salt, we must have forgotten it," I said.

"That's okay, we don't need it," Ken answered.

"Where's the plates?" Harvey asked.

"In the same box as the fry pan, and hurry; these eggs are getting black around the edge," Ken informed us.

A search through the box of pans and other cooking gear produced the plates.

"Get something to take them out of the fry pan," Ken said with a little panic in his voice.

Again a frantic search was started for the spatula. Meanwhile the eggs continued to cook and the black edges were now extending into the yoke.

"Hurry, these eggs are DONE!" Ken yelled as he scraped them from the pan and placed them on the plates.

"Think we'll want more?" Ron asked.

"Sure," I said.

The pan was filled again and this time they didn't get quite so well done and looked a little more appetizing. Breakfast finished, the scramble started for the cane poles and worms as we headed for the lake.

"Boy we better be careful with this new boat; it's the

first time we've used it," I cautioned.

Mother had purchased a new redwood boat at Montgomery Wards in Hastings. We climbed in and were soon fishing in our favorite spot. A few fish were caught and as the sun climbed higher in the sky the warmth of its rays felt good on our chilled bodies. The enthusiasm for fishing started to wane as each of us yawned and our movements slowed to a snail's pace; lack of sleep was taking its toll. Soon, exhausted and sleepy, we were back on shore and headed for the tent for a long overdue rest. The sun was high in the morning sky and its warm rays heated the tent to a balmy temperature; at last we were warm.

Awakening, we were hungry, so we started a fire and cleaned the fish. Carefully we rolled them in flour and placed them in the fry pan, which was much too hot. The grease spattered as the moisture steamed and popped.

"We better have something more than fish," I said.

"Let's open some beans," Ron suggested.

So the can was opened and poured into a separate pan. Someone peeled and diced onions and mixed them into the beans. The pan was then placed close to the fire. As they simmered away, we continued to fry fish. Now all was ready. We transferred the fish to our plates. Some were black on one side and others fried to perfection. Of course the beans had never been stirred, so they were burnt on the side next to the fire and the remainder was stone cold. Still we ate heartily. After all, we reasoned, we're camping! We hadn't expected to be able to cook as well as Mother.

Lunch was finished and the dirty dishes were placed with those from breakfast, making an impressive pile. No one mentioned washing them.

"Think we should get wood in for night?" I asked.

"Be a good idea. We sure don't want to do what we did last night," Ken answered.

After about an hour, the woodpile was sufficient for a couple days.

"Let's go fishin'!" Ken cried.

That evening, Dad came to the lake to see how we had survived the first night and day. Seeing everything was okay, he told us, "I have a few things your mother sent."

She had fixed a meal, and it sure was better than what we had eaten all day! We passed the evening around the campfire. Darkness was setting in as we dragged our tired bodies into the tent and drifted off to sleep. Morning came too soon for the four of us as we staggered from the bedrolls and out for breakfast. Looking around for dishes, we found to our amazement that there were none clean.

The first order of the day then was to wash dishes. A fire was started and soon the water we had carried from the lake was steaming hot. Dish washing began, but the dried egg on yesterday's breakfast plates just didn't want to give up that yellow look. Likewise, the congealed lard and flour had formed something that resembled mud in the frying pan. The water cooled, and no amount of scrubbing seemed to loosen the hardened mess. Next the pan that was used for beans was placed in the dishpan. One side was caked hard with a black coating that resembled burnt carbon; it was what remained of the beans.

"Maybe if we get some sand to scrub with it might help," I said.

"Or maybe a stone," Ken came back.

Both methods were employed and after considerable work the dishes, though not much cleaner, were pronounced washed.

"Boy, we better wash dishes as soon as we finish eating this time."

Now we were really ready for breakfast. The food for today, fish. The frying process finished, we took them out to find they weren't quite done to perfection; the fry pan still popped hot grease. The flour in it as well as the fish were both burnt but the end result was better than the day before. The lure of the fish poles beckoned, so we left our dishes and took off to the lake, leaving behind our resolve to wash dishes immediately after each meal!

The week continued and evenings usually brought Dad and Mother to check us. They were always welcome, since they brought with them a hearty meal. We had caught more fish than we could possibly eat, so we brought up our burlap bag of fish from the lake and poured the extras into Dad's pail for him to take home.

The weekend came all too soon and Harry Fennis, who was soon to be Aunt Helen Miles's husband, came from Lansing, and knowing we would be at the lake with lots of bait, he had planned to buy his worms there, rather than drive the extra two miles to get them at the house. Stopping at our camp he asked if he could buy a hundred worms.

"Sure," I said, "Fifty cents!

"But they're only twenty-five cents at the house, why fifty cents here?" Harry asked.

"If you want the twenty-five-cent worms you have go to the house to get them. At the lake they're fifty cents," I stated.

Harry just laughed and paid the exorbitant price. This became a private joke between Uncle Harry and me the rest of our lives. Nearly sixty years later as Uncle Harry lay too sick to sit up we reminisced about those fifty-cent worms. I told him that if I had to deliver worms to heaven, they would be a dollar per hundred! We both laughed as the tears rolled down our cheeks; we both knew the end was near.

The week of camping and fishing was over, the tent was rolled up, and the camping gear packed as we waited for Dad to come pick us up. It had been a good week, we had learned a lot, except for one thing: the timely washing of dishes.

The Big Fish and Little Goat

Little Bill and I finished the morning milking and put the cows out to pasture.

"Let's go pike fishing," Little Bill suggested.

Little Bill had been working for Roy Preston, a farmer in the neighborhood, every day the weather permitted, so his time to fish had been sharply curtailed. Roy had purchased a hay baler, something still new for our area, and between cuttings of his own hay he did custom baling for the neighboring farmers. The baler required three people to operate it: one to run the tractor and two to poke and tie wires to form bales. Little Bill had the hot and dirty job of poking wires but he didn't mind because he was making money. Today was his day off and we were soon headed for Lower Lake. This was my first chance to use my brand-new casting rod and reel and I carried it proudly. When we reached the lake, we jumped in the boat and pushed off, throwing our lines in the water shortly thereafter and hoping for that BIG fish. Bill put a red and white daredevil spoon on his line and I put on a brass spoon with two red beads for eyes.

"I got one!" Little Bill shouted.

Sure enough, in just a few minutes he had a small pike in the boat. Then I had something on, fought it for a short time, and landed a fish myself. It wasn't a pike, but a dogfish.

"We don't want that thing, just kill it and throw it back," Little Bill commanded.

"How should I do that?" I asked.

"Well just cut it open!" Little Bill instructed.

I took out my pocketknife and cut the fish's head off and threw it overboard. Fishing resumed and soon we had four nice pike. We were now about halfway around the lake and I made a cast near some weeds close to shore. I saw a swirl in the water as a fish started for my lure. Seeing it I jerked the lure from the water.

"Why did ya do that?" barked Little Bill.

"I don't want that fish on my line or in this boat; it looked long as a boat oar going through the water," I remarked sternly.

"It couldn't have been that big, maybe three feet," Little Bill came back.

"It looked bigger than that, besides it was bigger then I want in this boat with me!" I assured him.

Little Bill continued to give me a hard time as we went back to fishing. We'd had great success already that day: four pike, one dogfish, and many strikes, as well as several hooked that we hadn't been able to land. There was a splash. "Oh no!" I shouted.

"What happened?" Little Bill questioned with disgust in his voice.

"I just lost my fishing pole!" I cried out.

"Well, how'd you manage that?" Little bill came back.

"I went to cast, and the spoon caught on the side of the boat and it jerked it right outta my hands and into the lake!" I said.

My new rod and reel was now in about twelve feet of water and the lake bottom was mud.

"Don't get all upset—I'll dive down and get it for you," Little Bill said.

Stripping off all his clothes, Little Bill dove down. Kicking hard he reached the bottom, but his strokes stirred up the sediment and he was unable to see anything. He returned to the surface and repeated the dives several times, feeling around the bottom since he couldn't see a thing. None of these attempts produced the rod. Sadly we gave up and headed home. I was very upset with myself.

The next morning, our hopes of finding the rod renewed, Bill Barber and Little Bill made a large hook and tied it to a long rope to drag the lake bottom. We hoped to latch on to some line or the pole itself. Everything ready we headed out. We rowed to the area where the pole had gone down, and the dragging operation commenced. It lasted well into the afternoon, to no avail—the pole was gone forever! Giving up, we headed home as it was getting close to time for chores.

Once home, Little Bill yelled to Ken. "It's milking time, better climb up the windmill and watch for cars so we can get the cows across the road."

Scurrying up, Ken perched himself on the top of the ladder to signal when it was all clear to open the gate and head the cows across the road to the barnyard. After we got the cows in their stanchions and the milking under way, Ken came into the barn and was teasing the cats. They had gathered to drink the milk we were squirting at them. They were very proficient drinking the stream of milk that came their way. One kitten started toward the new cow that was known to kick.

Ken reached down to get the cat just as the cow let fly with her hind foot catching Ken squarely on the side of his head, sending him back against the cement wall. The cat scurried away, and Ken lay on the floor stunned. Little Bill jumped off his milk stool and reached Ken just as he started to get up. We were very frightened as we took the crying Ken to the house and related the story to Mother. Her close check determined no serious damage had been done, so Little Bill and I returned to the barn to finish chores.

We took the milk to the house and strained it through a cloth. Every night we put some of it aside for table use, and the remainder we put through the separator.

This was usually Ken's job, but that evening we had to fill in for him. The old hand-crank machine separated the cream from the skim milk, which we put in a special cream can and chilled in the refrigerator. We used the skim milk mixed with ground grain for pig feed. This finished the chores, and we were free for the evening.

That evening, Dad and Mother had called Grampa and Gramma to the kitchen.

"We have something to tell you," Dad said.

With a little bewilderment in their faces my elderly grandparents stood silent.

"My dad is coming to live with us, so we'll need more room," explained Mother. And, after a long pause, "We just bought you a house trailer to live in. It's not very large, but it's yours as long as you want it. The trailer is just large enough for a sofa bed and a small dinning table with benches attached to the walls. There's a small kitchen area, with a round cast-iron coal-burning stove for heat."

Grampa sat down on the wooden kitchen chair with tears of joy trickling down his cheeks. Gramma just stood there in disbelief.

The next day, the trailer was brought home and set up. An overhead electric power line was run to the trailer. Plans were made for a fence to be placed around two sides to block out a section of the barnyard. Grampa put his ice-fishing shanty in one corner of their yard to use for outside storage. In another corner, he built a large box and covered it with rolled roofing, to keep coal in. The coal was for use in their small cast-iron heating stove. With Grampa and Gramma settled into their new trailer home, we spent many an evening with them playing cards and checkers. Often it would be packed with the five of us kids either playing games or listening to Grampa's yarns, as he puffed on his pipe filled with Union Leader tobacco. Swirls of smoke streamed upward to the ceiling as he spun tales of the past. With his unique way of suspense and drama, he kept us kids spellbound. Euchre and pinochle were the games of choice and in the summer they could go until the wee hours of the morning.

During long evening sessions Gramma would sometimes bake a molasses dripping pan cake. She'd send one of us to get fresh cream to be whipped into soft peaks as a topping for the hot cake. The games and stories would be interrupted while the cake was devoured.

Grampa was in charge of the heat when it was needed to take the chill off the cool evenings or to keep it warm in the winter. He'd stoke up the little cast-iron potbelly stove with coal, always making more fire than needed, and we'd have to open the windows and door to make it comfortable inside. Memory built upon memory and we stored them each in our minds to be recalled and cherished over and over and over again throughout the years.

There was a man in the neighborhood who was

known to all of us kids as Billy Goat Brown. Mr. Brown was a bachelor and he raised goats. He asked Ken one day while they were talking if he'd like to have a goat. Having only one udder she would never be profitable for milking. Ken readily accepted and came home with Nanny. Almost immediately she became a real menace to Mother and Grampa.

Now goats like to get up as high as they can, and Grampa's coal box was the highest point around that she could get on. The nanny would run and jump up onto the top, her sharp hoofs cutting through the roofing. Out would come Grampa with a broom, and run her off just to have her return a few minutes later and repeat the whole episode.

Our Grandpa Miles said that goats could be taught to pull a wagon. So with his help I began to build a wagon and harness. After several days of hard work, we finished the wagon and were ready to test it. We put the harness on the goat, hitched her to the wagon and I started to get in. Ken came along at just that moment. He stated emphatically that since the goat was his, not mine, he should be the one to drive. Now, he hadn't helped in any way with all of the preparations, and so an argument erupted.

I stalked off with the harness complaining, "It's my harness and my wagon. I built them and you're not going to use either one!" I took the axe and chopped the harness into little pieces. No one drove the goat that day or ever again!

Mother's problem with the goat centered around Nanny's fondness for rose bushes; she considered the full blooms a real delicacy. She was very efficient at stripping the blooms off the trellis, leaving just a very few on the underside. This led to her demise. She also tried to eat the washing as it hung on the line to dry. She tormented the dog by staying just out of his reach past the end of his chain, where she'd prance around in front of him until he got all worked up and barked furiously. She really got Dad's attention by jumping onto the hood of the car, climbing to the very top, and scratching the paint with her sharp hooves. Sometime later, a man came to the house and asked to purchase Nanny. Dad didn't have to think about it twice. She was gone!

Our troubles forgotten, Ken and I fashioned an old wringer washer into a holding tank for turtles, frogs, and anything else we caught and desired to keep. It had a constant turnover of animal life. One particular day, we decided to head for Lower Lake and get a fresh supply of small turtles. The lake was a haven for them, but a dangerous place for kids. In fact, using a cane fish pole it was possible to push its complete length through the root-laden moss and bog that made up the shore. There was nothing but water beneath the entanglement, and jumping on the mass would produce a wave in the shoreline for several feet in all directions.

Pushing the boat into the water, we began the hunt.

The muck area just a few feet to the west side of the boat landing was soupy enough to row in, yet thick enough that the turtles could actually lie on it without sinking. As I rowed and Ken grabbed, it wasn't long before the boat bottom was crawling with a nice variety of turtles of various sizes. There were small painted turtles, rubberbacks, and even small snappers.

"Tom, turn the boat this way; there's a bunch over there," Ken instructed.

Excited about how easy it was, Ken lunged to get some more. Now, experience is the best teacher, and we were about to gain a little more common sense! Splash, Ken fell into the lake.

Thrashing around in that black murky water trying to stay afloat, he yelled, "Grab me!"

I jumped up from the middle seat where I'd been rowing, stepped to the front, and grabbed his arm. Both of us struggled to haul him back into the safety of the boat. He was black from head to toe with that mucky, black, stinking water.

"What'll we do now?" he questioned.

"Well, we sure can't go home like this!" I exclaimed.

Silence followed as we thought about our problem.

"Let's go out in the deep water and I'll jump in and swim around 'til my clothes are clean," Ken said.

I rowed out to the deep water and Ken slid overboard. Hanging on to the side of the boat, he pushed himself up and down as the water turned black all around him. "It's working. Keep going 'til you're clean. Jump up and down fast and I'll scrub you wherever the old mud doesn't come off," I said.

Soon he looked somewhere near respectable, and with my help, he climbed into the boat. "We got to stay here 'til I'm dry. Ma would know what happened and would never let us come alone again," Ken cautioned.

"I know, but it's so hot today it shouldn't take long," I agreed

We were soon able to head for home with our bucket of turtles. Once there, we placed them in the old washer and went about our play and didn't mention a word to anyone about falling in. The evidence had been completely washed away, and we saved Mother the worry about what might happen when we would again travel into another adventure. That night when Ken undressed he found his once-white underwear was stained to a dark, dingy gray. In fact, it was nearly black! Slipping them into the dirty-clothes basket without being seen, we were home free—until wash day anyway.

Summer was over, school started, and Ken and I began looking forward to trapping season. Dad had told us we could trap Lower Lake if we could get permission. Old Dan Straben gave us the okay, and with our traps ready, we could hardly wait. Now we were not yet proficient trappers, but we were capable of getting a few muskrats. It was hard to make sets on the soft, muck shore, so we would have to devise our own method of trapping.

"There's a runway," Ken remarked, pointing to depression in the mud.

"Looks like it goes right up to that hole," I said

"Ya but how we gonna set a trap in this old mud; it'll just sink," Ken remarked.

"Let's put it right in the hole," I suggested.

"Dad said that's not legal!" Ken came back.

"Well, how else we gonna set a trap? Nobody ever comes around here anyway. You cut a stake and I'll set the trap," I said.

"Make sure you get it way up in the hole so's no one will see it!" Ken instructed.

One afternoon in December, while running our trap lines along the south shore of the lake, we observed a lone ice fisherman just off shore where some of our more notorious trap sets had been made. This should have been a tipoff, as we knew the fishing was no good where this guy sat. We worked around the shoreline inspecting each of our traps. The fisherman kept watching. When we were about ready to leave he stood up and started toward us.

"It's the game warden!" I yelled.

Throwing away what traps we had in our hands we started running through the brush and into the woods. In a panic and panting, we ran out the opposite side and across the fields, making a big circle toward home.

Now if the game warden had really wanted to get us, he would have followed the tracks we left in the snow, but this thought never crossed our minds. Our only thought was to get out of there and home. When we finally made it back, we quietly went about our chores as if nothing unusual had happened!

Later I went to Grampa and Gramma's trailer and struck up a conversation with Grampa. He sat back on the sofa, reached over to fill his pipe from the large Union Leader tobacco can, and carefully packed the tobacco into it just right. Touching the flame from his lighter to it, he drew hard, until the tobacco glowed red. He puffed away, sending smoke rings upward, and began one of his famous stories. I struggled to keep my mind on the story. Fragments of it mingled with thoughts of what would happen if we got caught, and they tangled together in my mind.

Suddenly, a strange car pulled in the driveway. It was the same color and had the same sloped back as the game warden's, and my heart pounded! I was sure he'd come to take Ken and me off to jail. I stared out the window, my eyes glued to the car, as the door opened and out stepped—one of Dad's friends, what a relief!

Ken and I had almost forgotten about our day's adventure when just shortly after dark, we heard the sound of sleigh bells in the driveway. Mrs. Newton had hitched her mules to an open bobsled, loaded up her girls, and stopped to see if any of us wanted to join them. We all eagerly jumped aboard and were off. The ride took us up and down the hills of a side road nearby, singing and laughing as we went. Sleigh rides with Mrs. Newton and her team of mules could last two or three hours, and we loved every minute.

Rabbits and Squirrels

The war had been raging about a year when Christmas morning dawned. Uncle Harry Miles Jr. was in the South Pacific fighting the Japanese, and his absence damped our joy. Even the large holiday meal in preparation, the roast goose and all the trimmings, had lost some of its appeal. One of our family was in harm's way, and there was a threat that several more would follow. Dad, who was trying to get his mind on something more pleasant, shouted, "Let's go hunting!"

Ken and I were eager and willing to do just that very thing, but Little Bill declined. Dad grabbed his single-barrel sixteen-gauge shotgun along with a handful of shells.

"Get your coats and let's go!" Dad said.

We crossed the road into the pasture and headed for the pond. The tall grasses and cattails around it were sure to contain a rabbit or two. Just as we stepped into the heavy grass, a rabbit flushed and ran up the slight incline to the corner of the field. Dad raised his gun and fired, a clean miss. He hurried to reload and fire again before the rabbit was out of range. Putting his thumb over the hammer and cocking it as he raised it to his shoulder, the gun fired but the rabbit kept running. His thumb had slipped off the hammer and allowed it to fire prematurely.

At that precise moment a limb on the old oak tree in the corner of the pasture dropped to the ground. Ken and I stared at the tree, then broke into laughter. "Dad you shot a limb out of the tree! You're supposed to aim lower. The rabbit was on the ground!" we cried out. We all had a good laugh while the rabbit ran safely out of sight. The hunt that day didn't put any rabbits on the table, but it sure did put memories in our hearts that have lasted a lifetime.

Dad shared many more hunts with us boys and plenty of game was taken, including rabbits, pheasants, ducks, and squirrels. But no hunt was more favorably remembered than that one. Besides the camaraderie, our spirits were lifted, and the glum thoughts of war abandoned

As we grew older all three of us boys carried guns, and hunting under Dad's guidance rapidly diminished. His time was being consumed by work in the factory. Little Bill took over as the self-appointed instructor and disciplinarian—a roll he enjoyed, and which he actually did very well. Bill Barber often joined us, and the four of us hunted regularly with one another.

October 15th marked the beginning of small-game hunting season. Every year we took a day's vacation from school to hunt. There was pheasant hunting in the morning and evening, while squirrels were the prey during the day. Little Bill and I gained considerable experience hunting in the wetlands one fall during duck season. A wood lot near the house had flooded, and the ducks were plentiful.

We walked into the section and took several unsuccessful shots while stalking. We found ourselves on the opposite side of the pond from home. The pond covered a large area and required several minutes to walk around. Little Bill suggested we walk the woven wire fence that went straight through the middle of the pond. This would save us walking all the way around, and lots of time and trouble.

The sun was setting, the temperature was dropping fast, and frost was in the night air. Little Bill started by climbing up the fence about a foot off the ground. Testing, he stepped sideways along it above the water.

"It gonna work, so come on," Little Bill called.

We held on to the fence with one hand and our guns in the other. We proceeded across the cold pond according to plan until we found ourselves in deeper water and had to climb higher up the fence. Thus we worked our way along, until the water under us was over two feet deep leaving very little fence protruding above the water line.

As we stepped up one more wire the fence started to sway back and forth, the top bending low toward the water. Attempting to counter this we leaned back and the fence sprang back going much too far the other way! Things were becoming serious as the bouncing back and forth continued. We yelled at each other to slow down, but neither could. Suddenly there was a loud snap as one of the old wooden fence posts, rotted from many years of weathering, broke! We both found ourselves lying on our backs in frigid water, holding our guns high to try to keep them dry. We jumped up, water splashing in all directions.

"Wow, that was cold," stuttered Little Bill with his teeth chattering, trying to compose himself. "That wasn't too good an idea was it? We got to get home and fast!"

We hurried off stomping our way through the muddy waist-deep water until we reached shore and good footing. Once on dry ground we ran to keep warm until we reached the house where we pealed off our partially frozen clothes and hurried to get into dry ones. We snuggled next to the stove where we spent a good long time basking in the warmth of the fire. There were lots of hunts to come, but Little Bill and I never had one quite as chilling as this.

Soon Little Bill allowed me to hunt alone. He figured I needed a bit more instruction though before Ken and I were ready to hunt together without him. One afternoon I started for the squirrel woods to the west of the house. I carried Dad's sixteen-gauge single-shot gun under my arm. Walking into the woods as quietly as possible, I sat down and leaned back against a tree. I waited patiently for a squirrel to show itself and suddenly one jumped through the branches over my head. Leaves dry from the fall frost rattled, giving away the position of the squirrel. I stood up to shoot, but every time I moved the squirrel would go to the other side of the tree! I tried walking around the tree but the squirrel scampered to the other side. I know, I thought, I'll just get close to the trunk and look around.

The idea worked fine I could see the squirrel, flattened out against the trunk, listening for movement on the ground. Looking straight up, I twisted my body very quietly around the trunk and cocked the old sixteen-gauge as I raised it to my shoulder. What a shot this would make! The squirrel was just six or seven feet from the end of the barrel.

I squeezed off the shot, and being of a slight build, the recoil knocked my twelve-year-old eyes completely off the target. I recovered quickly enough to see the squirrel fly through the air and land a good fifty feet from the tree. Slightly shaken, but proud, I stood, and straightened my shoulders. I walked to retrieve the first game I had bagged totally by myself. What I found, unfortunately, was not so much a squirrel as a well-worn piece of hide holding squirrel tail to squirrel head. The blast had removed all of its body parts. The first common-sense lesson of hunting is that game must be more than a few feet from the muzzle of the gun.

After a few weeks, Little Bill figured my instruction was complete so he left Ken to hunt with me, while he hunted with the older neighborhood boys. At ten and twelve years of age, Ken and I weren't what you might call seasoned hunters. We were usually careful, and had a great love for the sport. Together we soon learned where the game was likely to be and a few tricks to spook them out.

Winter set in and rabbit hunting was in full swing. Guns over our shoulders and well padded with heavy clothing, we started for Lower Lake. It was time to have a try at these furry little animals. The deep grass along the shore was prime rabbit habitat. Now, we had fished and trapped the lake many a time, and so we knew that the shore was anything but safe. If you stepped in the wrong place you could break right through the boggy root cover and sink out of sight. We figured if we were careful, we could just jump from one bog to another.

It wasn't long before the excitement of the chase overwhelmed our caution. Ken missed a jump, and found himself in the black muck up to his waist. Quickly he placed his gun across the two bogs, held on, and yelled, "Tom I'm sinking."

I ran to his aid and we both struggled to free him from the sucking muck. Finally, we got him out and he stretched out across the ground. He was soaked to the skin with the black goo, and his gun was covered with muck too. So much for that hunt! We abandoned the chase and headed home, Ken slogging along in yet another set of gray-black clothes. Some more common sense learned the hard way.

The war years continued and more family members left for service. Dad's brother, Lester, shipped out to Europe and Dad and Mother were appointed guardians of his five children. His youngest was a daughter, Cora Ione, whom we renamed Joyce, and she was only about six weeks old. Since there were five kids in our house, Grampa and Gramma went to Uncle Lester's house to care for his children there. Soon little Joyce was transferred back to our house to ease the load on our aging grandparents. It was a long time before Lester came home from the war. Mother and Dad were the only parents Joyce had ever known, so Uncle Lester let her stay with us. Dad and Mother adopted her later.

Dad's long hours of factory work, and Mother's hard work caring for her family, plus the added burden of the extended family, took its toll on our parents. Still in their mid-thirties, they started looking older and more tired. The war was changing our family. We could no longer be isolated and shielded from the world or the war. Five close family members were serving in the military, and all in combat areas. I kept in contact with each by letter. It was a great comfort to receive the correspondence from them, and to know they were still safe. Dad's brothers, Ike and Lester, served in Europe. Mother brother Harry served in the South Pacific, and her brother Louis served as a tail gunner on a B-17 out of England. Uncle Harry Fennis served as an infantry-man in Europe.

Little Bill had now grown into a young man, Vera was in high school, and Francis no longer thought tag-ging along with her brothers was fun. Ken and I did most of the gardening and barn chores. I also worked for the farmers in the area, officially driving a team of horses, though most of the time, I merely held the reigns while the horses went about their work.

The little clan was growing up. Nothing brought this home more than when, at the age of seventeen, Little Bill enlisted in the navy. He was off to war in the Pacific. The remaining four were crushed and worried that the era of innocence was now truly over.

The Tribute

December 12, 1994, I had just finished Dad's funeral message on this typical winter day. It had not been easy. I had to be strong throughout the ordeal, but now it was over and it was my time to grieve. Returning to the room that held his flower-laden casket, I looked down the long aisle as thoughts ran rampant through my mind and the enormity of my loss swept over me. For over sixty-three years I had never been without a parent. Suddenly I was the oldest living son. This day put to rest an era that spanned over eighty-seven years.

Dad had met and overcome many trials, but in the end, death comes to us all. Years of smoking had taken their toll, and lung cancer kills. For the last six months all of us remaining children had taken turns, a week or so at a time, staying in his home so that his last days could be spent with his family. Now it was finished. I walked up to the casket and, leaning on the edge, I placed my hand on the cold stiff arm of what was once a vibrant living person.

Just four years before, our family had come to this very same room, and not just once. Twice within three months we were there to commemorate the lives of Little Bill, who had died of a heart attack, and his wife Doris, who succumbed to cancer. A heart attack had taken Mother twelve years earlier. Yet, my thoughts were not all sorrowful. As a child I had followed after this man, asking questions and talking a mile a minute. His wisdom and teachings followed me all my life, and made me the person I am. Looking down on the motionless form, I couldn't help thinking that a great man lay there before me. And yet he was not great as the world counts greatness.

He did nothing to change the course of history. He hadn't done much to change events in our own community. Oh, he had served on the county school board, worked on community projects, and helped his neighbors, but nothing earth-shaking. He had educated himself in home study, and worked up to supervision at his job. But none of this seemed important now. What counted was that he had been a good father. He provided the best he could, often sacrificing of himself for the good of his family. He and Mother opened their home to others many times. Dad always said that as long as he had a roof over his head and food on the table, so would all of his extended family. And his life proved that he meant it.

Fond memories flooded my thoughts. "Oh dad, you did it again!" I could hear Vera say, as she bit into a good-looking slice of toast—on the top anyway. Dad and his Sunday morning oven toast!

"Dad you shot the limb out of the tree!" Ken and I had shouted as he had tried to get a second shot at a rabbit during one of our many hunting experiences.

He taught us to hunt safely, a sport I still enjoy today. He also passed on his passion for fishing and trapping, and his love for the outdoors. His influence molded us forever. I remembered mending fence with him, when I was so small that I was nothing more than a bother. Yet, he patiently helped me along. That was his way. Later, memories of hunting and fishing together as a family filled my mind. I had sought his counsel in the decisions of life, and in later days I gained wisdom from him as we sat and just talked. Memories were all I had left now of this man who had given us so much. He lived to see all his children through to middle age, then into retirement.

Little Bill worked all his life at the same factory where Dad was employed, and died young. Sadly, he and Doris had accumulated wealth, but were childless. One thing Little Bill did leave was great childhood memories. Catching pigeons, poking at skunks, and crossing ponds on a wire fence, life was never dull for us kids with his leadership.

Vera spent most of her work life as village clerk in Lake Odessa. She and her husband, Donavon (Doc) had one daughter, Lou Anne, and two grandchildren.

I had worked as an industrial engineer. With my wife

Sue and our children, we operated a farm of one hundred twenty acres. Later we owned and operated a sporting goods store (Tom's Tackle Shop) in Ionia, Michigan. We have four children, Karen, Doctor Tom, Pamela, and Nancy, and now fourteen grandchildren.

Kenneth worked in a factory for several years. At the same time he and his wife, Evelyn, started a business manufacturing fishing tackle (K & E Tackle). They have three children, Kathy, Ken Jr., and James, and four grandchildren.

Francis and her husband, Paul (now deceased), had three children, Vicky, Debra, and Michael, and five grandchildren. While her children were young, Fran became a registered nurse. Later in life she married Bill Wallace.

Joyce and her husband Jack had no children. Both worked at various jobs near Kalamazoo, Michigan.

Dad and Mother could be proud; their children were all successful. All of their sons had served their country; Bill in the Navy during the second World War, I in the Air Force during the Korean war, and Kenneth in the Army also during the Korean War.

As I stood there, the time had finally come to close this chapter of life. The room was empty except for me and my dad. Gripping his arm I said, "Goodbye Dad, see you and Mother in heaven." Though they were good people; both had come to realize that no human has or could live a life totally free of sin. Sensing Jesus's great love for them and their need of forgiveness, both had asked Him to forgive their sins and be their savior, Mom just four days before her death and Dad about six months later. He lived and practiced a growing faith for the nearly twelve years before his death.

Little Bill became a believer the night mother died, and my prayer is that all the family will do the same. As I let go of Dad's arm, I knew I was releasing him for the last time in this life. It was hard, but I turned and walked silently out of the room. The depth of this loss encompassed me; never again would I seek his wisdom or his company in this life. And yes, never again would we need to be there for him at his most vulnerable times, as in the loss of Mother, or in this last sickness. We had all done our best for him, and as I passed through the door into the great hall, I realized it was over. A new era had begun.

I'll always cherish the memories of yesteryear with Mother and Dad, as they struggled to make ends meet. I'll remember those times with Grandfather Libby and Grandmother Bessie, playing card games and eating dripping pan cake as we listened to the tall tales. I'll also cherish the memory of the many adventures together with Little Bill, Vera, Kenneth and Francis. All of these events created a happy childhood in a time when children could be children, free to roam the countryside, be one with nature, and at peace with themselves and God.

The Great Depression was hard, but it developed a bond between the families that made up the rural communities. Neighbor looked out for neighbor, just because it was the right thing to do. It built character and a dependence on one another. It developed imagination, ingenuity and a sense of value for life and possessions. It was not a throwaway society. Oh, for the peaceful days of that time. In comparison, innocence has been lost for many of today's children. They don't experience the pleasures of a true childhood. Those of us who knew better times can only wait and pray that the fast-and-now generation will realize that money, fancy cars, big houses, and careers do not bring lasting happiness. These things are necessary in moderation, but in excess they bring only a desire for more, increasing the tempo of a self-destructive life.

True happiness comes from within and by the grace of God. It is available to anyone regardless of circumstance. Search it out and take time to smell the roses, for they only last a few days.

"For all flesh is as grass,
and all the glory of man as the flower of grass.
The grass withereth,
and the flower thereof falleth away."
I Peter 1:24

At the present I must wait, but, by His grace, our little clan may again be united with Mother and Dad in glory.

Memories

How long has it been? Memories now still.

Our hair is gray, our strength has faded.
We rock in our chair, a calm message is stated.
"Time is short, give your cares to me,
come close and rest."
We put it off. "Not now."
Knowing we're missing the test.
He calls again, "I'm the judge! You cannot win!
Take my free grace and find peace within."

"It's over!" the cry. If yielded to Him,
the best will begin.

How long will it be before memories
of us will grow dim?

About the Author

Tom Sprague was reared in rural Barry County, Michigan during the Great Depression of the 1930s. He still lives with his wife of 56 years, on the farm purchased in 1955, just six miles from his birthplace. Tom and his wife attended a one-room country school through the eighth grade before going to a consolidated high school.

Tom served four years in the United States Air Force during the Korean War. During his military service and after returning home he attended college. Tom then worked as an Industrial Engineer before starting a full-line sporting goods retail business in 1968.

In 1974, Tom was elected to the *Who's Who in Michigan* in the field of business and economics. In 1983 he sold his business and retired. Still too young to call it quits, he started a part-time accounting business that soon became full time. He retired again at age 62. Tom then wrote his book from *Poverty to Glory*.

Tom and his wife now spend their leisure time traveling, hunting, and fishing throughout North America.